CARB MANAGER'S
keto diet
COOKBOOK

The Easiest Way to **Lose Weight Fast** with
101 Recipes That You Can Track with **QR Codes**

Carb Manager®
The #1 Ketogenic Diet App
Written by Mandy Davis

Photography by Becky Winkler

PAGE STREET
PUBLISHING CO.

PAGE STREET
PUBLISHING CO.

Copyright © 2020 Carb Manager

First published in 2020 by

Page Street Publishing Co.

27 Congress Street, Suite 105

Salem, MA 01970

www.pagestreetpublishing.com

Distributed by Macmillan, sales in Canada by The Canadian Manda Group.

24   23   22   21   20   2   3   4   5   6

ISBN-13: 978-1-64567-144-2

ISBN-10: 1-64567-144-5

Library of Congress Control Number: 2019957318

Cover and book design by Molly Gillespie for Page Street Publishing Co.

Photography by Becky Winkler

Printed and bound in the United States

To all the loyal users of Carb Manager—
thank you for your support for the past 10 years.

contents

Satisfying Sides 157

Savory Snacks 187

Sweets & Fat Bombs 217

introduction

Welcome to the official Carb Manager cookbook! My husband Kevin and I started the Carb Manager app in 2010, when we were living in rural Hawaii. We both loved to eat and cook, and we fantasized about an easy way to track what we ate.

As Carb Manager developed, we listened to our community, who taught us so much about low-carb diets in general, and keto in particular. We added features for tracking intermittent fasting, logging exercises, calculating net carbs and other macronutrients (macros) and much more. Fast forward to today, and Carb Manager is the most popular and top-rated low-carb and keto diet app, loved by hundreds of thousands of people around the world.

While it is easy to start most diets on your own, sticking to any lifestyle change is almost impossible without a community. One of my first responsibilities at Carb Manager was managing customer support. While I could help on the technical side, I often found myself referring people to our discussion groups. There they would find a community of people struggling with the same questions: How long does it actually take to lose 50 pounds? What if my family refuses to eat keto? How much water do I need to drink? What are your favorite recipes? How can I make this easier? The community was always positive and supportive, and the messages I heard repeated there helped shape the Carb Manager mantras: Everything takes time. Be easy on yourself. You can do it.

After many requests, we started adding original recipes to Carb Manager in 2017 and connected with our three amazing keto recipe developers, Amanda, Jessica and Emma, with whom I worked to develop this cookbook. We have included a handful of "greatest hits" from the Carb Manager app and website, so if you're a fan of the Philly Cheesesteak Skillet or Thai Spicy Peanut Chicken with Asian Slaw, please turn to pages 94 and 73! In total, you'll find more than 100 recipes that are easy to follow, delicious and have their net carbs and macros up front. Every recipe can be opened in the app by scanning the included QR code, so you can easily log all of your meals with a few taps. If you haven't downloaded the app, you will need to do so first.

Our number one goal is to help everyone eat delicious food that keeps them healthy and happy. Over the years, we've learned that low-carb cooking can be just as flavorful, nutritious and exciting as anything you've made before. Let's get cooking!

A Little Bit about Keto

Keto can refer to any diet that restricts carbohydrates such that a person goes into ketosis, meaning that they burn fat, or ketones, for fuel instead of carbohydrates. Typically this requires restricting your net carbs (total carbs minus fiber and sugar alcohols) to 5 percent of calories, or less than approximately 25 grams a day, depending on your daily caloric goal. Fat intake is increased to about 70 percent of calories, and protein fills in the remaining 25 percent of calories.

There are a few different approaches to keto. The most relaxed version is called "dirty keto," which means you can eat pretty much anything you want as long as you meet your goals for net carbs and macronutrients. On the flip side, there is "strict keto," which eliminates all sugar, grains, legumes, most fruits, starchy vegetables and all but high-fat dairy.

Carb Manager as a tool is officially neutral in approach— our members can use it any way they would like, even to track non-keto diets. We do, however, encourage people to eat sustainable meats and seafood and switch to healthy fats, for both dietary and environmental reasons.

A note for readers following strict keto diets: Our recipes, including those you'll find in this book, sometimes include seasonings in small amounts that may have sugar in them, like honey or Korean gochujang sauce. Occasionally, we include tomatoes, onions, carrots and other vegetables that people following strict keto may prefer to avoid. If you are strictly gluten free, you'll want to substitute tamari or liquid aminos for soy sauce. Please check the ingredients list and make appropriate substitutions.

Keto isn't a one-size-fits-all diet. Many of our members follow "cyclical keto," which means setting a higher net carb limit a few days a week. Others have seen success switching to a low-carb, high-fat (LCHF) plan, which means limiting net carbs to approximately 12 percent of calories, or under approximately 60 grams of net carbs a day. As a complement to this way of eating, we have also seen a growing interest in intermittent fasting and shortened eating windows, which may help with appetite suppression and calorie restriction.

Ingredient Tips

Keto is all about eating high-quality, nutrient-dense foods made from natural ingredients. You may have noticed "keto" bars, supplements and other specialty ingredients at your local grocery store. These might be helpful if you are looking for a quick fix, but nothing replaces the basic building blocks of fresh vegetables and high-quality fats and proteins. A few ingredients commonly used in keto cuisine are worth highlighting.

When you first switch to a keto diet, it's important to find something that mimics starch, but without the carbs. This will help you feel satisfied and ease the transition. Cauliflower stars in this arena, typically processed into rice, which can be done by hand, prepared with a food processor or purchased ready-made in the freezer section of many grocery stores. Shirataki noodles are a traditional Japanese noodle made from the konjac yam that are very low in calories and net carbs and can substitute for pasta. Zucchini can also be made into noodles, either spiraled or shaved with a peeler.

Avocados provide a quick source of healthy fat and can be used for snacks or as part of a more complex recipe. Most nuts are a great source of fat and protein. Of particular note are almonds and almond flour, the backbone for most keto baked goods. Dark leafy greens are very low in carbohydrates and packed with nutrients.

There are also three sugar alternatives that are occasionally used: erythritol, stevia and monk fruit–based sweeteners. For a further discussion of sweeteners, please see page 217.

You'll find a complete Pantry List on page 242, which will be helpful if you're just getting started cooking keto.

Icons

At the beginning of each recipe you may find one or more of these icons, so if you're looking for a fast recipe outside of the Quick & Easy chapter (page 53) or a keto vegetarian option, you can identify them quickly. Paleo is defined as having no dairy, artificial sweeteners (though some recipes make them optional), soy or grains.

30 Minutes or Less · Dairy Free · Paleo · Vegetarian · 6+ Grams Net Carbs

Serving Sizes

Most of the recipes in this cookbook serve four people. Occasionally we adjusted recipes to serve fewer people for a dish that was easier to make in smaller batches. A few recipes, like Chocolate Celebration Cake (page 225) and Chili Con Carne (page 122), are best made in large batches. For recipes with items that could easily be used as snacks or stored and eaten individually (like fat bombs, biscuits and pancakes), we gave the nutritional data for each item or grouped the items in units of around 100 calories. Check the recipe's sidebar if you are unsure how many portions it will make.

Q&A with Dietitian Anthony O'Neill, PT, DPT, RDN

Is keto a healthy way to eat?

The research as of early 2020 has suggested that people tend to improve in many important markers of health while following the ketogenic diet, though there is still a lot left to learn. Some important improvements have been seen in cardiovascular risk factors, including improved blood pressure, lipid profile, weight and waist circumference [1–3]. Other studies have demonstrated improvements in inflammation [2, 4, 5], cognitive function [6, 7] and daytime fatigue [8]. These are some of the most common problems affecting Americans today.

Additionally, something that really sets the ketogenic diet apart from other diets is that it seems to be especially good for decreasing abdominal obesity [9]—that pesky belly fat that is so hard to get rid of. This is especially important since waist circumference is a risk factor for many chronic diseases. Based on this information, keto appears to be healthy, at least in the short term.

I highly recommend including lots of keto-friendly vegetables and good, quality fats with every meal. It's even possible to follow plant-based keto or Mediterranean keto diets. No matter how you decide to do it, it is important to maintain regular check-ups with a physician and other licensed health professionals (such as a dietitian) while on the keto diet, especially if you have diabetes or any other health condition.

How quickly will I lose weight?

There is no exact answer to this question. It varies greatly from person to person and depends on many variables, such as body composition and activity level. Like on most weight-loss diets, people will lose a chunk of weight quickly—however, this initial weight loss is more from water weight than fat. After that, you'll likely lose weight at an average loss of one to two pounds per week, which is considered a healthy rate of weight loss. The law of calories in and calories out still applies on the keto diet. That means to make weight loss more efficient, you need to make sure you are not exceeding your individualized calorie limit. The Carb Manager app can help you determine how many calories you should consume per day. Additionally, exercising is important—activity burns calories—and building muscle increases your resting metabolic rate so that you burn more calories. Keeping your carbs low enough to maintain ketosis so your body can adapt to burning fat will also help.

How long should I stay on the keto diet?

It appears to take about 3 weeks for the body to become fully keto-adapted and to reap the full benefits of the keto diet [3, 10]. After that, you can begin to slowly reintroduce healthy carbs into your diet if you like or, if keto seems to be working well for you, you can continue on keto. It's likely safe to stay on it longer than 3 weeks [2], so beyond that, it's up to you. It is important to check in with a doctor regularly to make sure you're having a positive response to the diet. If you have any medical condition, talk with your doctor before trying keto, as it will not agree with certain medical conditions.

Will keto affect my cholesterol?

Yes—in a good way! Most research shows that keto will improve your cholesterol by decreasing triglycerides and increasing high-density lipoprotein (HDL) [1–3]. It's important to consider that your low-density lipoprotein (LDL) cholesterol (typically referred to as "bad cholesterol") may increase. However, low-carb diets appear to increase the concentration of a type of LDL known as large-sized LDL, which is known to be less related to cardiovascular disease than small, dense LDL [11]. Therefore, an increase in LDL may not be of concern. If LDL cholesterol is a concern of yours, be sure to follow up with a doctor for monitoring.

Is keto good for type 2 diabetes?

Keto appears to be very good for type 2 diabetes. Research has suggested that keto is great for increasing insulin sensitivity, improving blood glucose and decreasing glycated hemoglobin (HbA1C) in patients with diabetes [2]. If you have diabetes, it's important to work with a doctor, dietitian or other licensed health professional knowledgeable in diabetes and the ketogenic diet to be sure that it is done safely.

How will keto affect my exercise performance?

This depends heavily on the individual and what kind of exercise you are doing. When you first start keto, your body hasn't adjusted to using fat for energy, and your body needs a lot of energy to exercise. Therefore, your exercise performance may suffer in the beginning, especially if you do high-intensity, explosive exercise. However, research has suggested that exercise performance is not diminished in those who are keto-adapted, meaning their bodies have adapted to efficiently using fat for energy. This has been demonstrated in ultra-endurance runners [12], CrossFit trainees [13] and high-intensity interval training (HIIT) participants [14]. If you are interested in building significant muscle mass, or if you just don't feel like you have the energy you need to exercise, it might be a good idea to try cyclical keto, which is normal keto with a couple of high-carb days mixed in each week. Check the Carb Manager app for guidance in cyclical keto.

Author's Note

The content in this book is not medical advice and is intended for informational and educational purposes only. Always talk to your doctor before changing your diet.

meal planning & food logs

Planning ahead sets you up for keto success. Having a fridge full of keto snacks, knowing what you will eat for your next meal and ridding your pantry of any carb-loaded temptations can be the difference between sticking with the diet and going off track. Making food decisions all day can be exhausting, so we highly recommend that you sit down—either at the beginning of the week or every few days—and plan exactly what you will eat. It's far better to prepare when you are fed and rested than to wait until you're tired, hungry and there is a vending machine nearby with potato chips with your name printed on them.

In the Carb Manager app, we provide a variety of curated meal plans, a personalized meal plan generator and tools to easily build your own custom meal plans. If you'd like to use this cookbook to plan your meals by hand, we recommend that you first calculate your daily net carb limit and calorie allotment based on your weight, activity level and desired weight change. You can use the Carb Manager app on your phone or at CarbManager.com to determine your own personalized goals for calories, net carbs, fat and protein. Every recipe in this book has its net carbs and other macros listed up front, so keep a tally of those values. People typically find it difficult to fit in enough fat at first, so we recommend checking out our Savory Snacks chapter (page 187) and Sweets & Fat Bombs chapter (page 217) to find easy ways to increase your fat without adding extra carbs.

Sample 3-Day Menu Charts

Here are a few sample menus based on three different example users of Carb Manager, inspired by the typical profiles of people we see using Carb Manager. We have provided 3 days for each person for inspiration and to help you see exactly what a daily keto diet might look like. The menus have been designed so that they are typically slightly below the daily targets to allow a bit of wiggle room. All recipes are for one serving unless otherwise noted.

Rita is 40 years old and was recently told by her doctor that she is pre-diabetic and has elevated liver enzymes. She is 5' 5" (165 cm), goes on brisk walks several days a week and currently weighs 190 pounds (86 kg). She would like to lose 2 pounds (1 kg) a month. She has a daily calorie goal of 1,845 and, to stay in ketosis, should aim for 23 grams of carbs or fewer a day.

Eduardo is 57 years old and weighs 245 pounds (111 kg). He is 5' 11" (180 cm) and tries to work out several days a week. His goal is to lose 5 pounds (2.3 kg) a month. He has a daily calorie goal of 2,453 and, to stay in ketosis, should aim for 31 grams of carbs or fewer a day.

Shelly is 25 years old and weighs 140 pounds (63.5 kg). She is 5' 7" (170 cm) and works out regularly. She practices intermittent fasting and would like to maintain her body weight. She eats keto for increased energy and general health. She has a daily calorie goal of 2,112 and should aim for 26 grams of carbs or fewer a day.

Rita's 3-Day Meal Plan

	BREAKFAST	LUNCH	DINNER	SNACKS
DAY 1 22 g net carbs 1,785 calories	Blueberry-Lemon Pancakes (2 pancakes) (page 18) Two tablespoons (30 ml) of Lakanto maple-flavored syrup Vanilla Rooibos Tea with Cream Froth (page 47)	Creamy Shrimp and Wild Rice Risotto (page 57)	Chicken-Fried Steak Cutlets (page 89) Buttermilk Biscuit (page 158) plus 1 tablespoon (14 g) of butter Sheet Pan Zucchini (page 174)	Hazelnut Truffle Fat Bombs (2 truffles) (page 218)
DAY 2 19 g net carbs 1,800 calories	Mini Mean Green Quiches (page 31) Coffee with 2 tablespoons (30 ml) of cream	Deluxe Taco Salad (page 139)	Almond Flounder with Spanish Rice and Salsa (page 98)	Hazelnut Truffle Fat Bombs (2 truffles) (page 218) Guacamole Parmesan Cups (page 200)
DAY 3 23 g net carbs 1,802 calories	Egg and Spicy Rice Brunch Bowl (page 35) plus 2 table-spoons (24 g) of sour cream Iced Almond Matcha Latte (page 49)	Superfood Keto Salad (page 132)	Crispy Cajun Wings with Paprika Mayo (page 76) Parmesan-Roasted Tomatoes (page 182) Dreamsicle Mousse (page 240)	Cheddar Zucchini Crisps (page 192) Coconut, Lime and Raspberry Fat Bombs (page 222)

Eduardo's 3-Day Meal Plan

	BREAKFAST	LUNCH	DINNER	SNACKS
DAY 1 32 g net carbs 2,384 calories	Bacon, Cheese and Watercress Omelette (page 36) Coffee with 2 tablespoons (30 ml) of cream	Chorizo and Shrimp Fajitas (page 54)	Lamb Kebab Meatball Plate (2 servings) (page 90) Peanut Butter and Jelly Ice Cream (page 235)	Almond Fat Bomb Fudge (page 221) Meat and Cheese Rolls (Mozzarella Cheese and Salami Rolls; page 207)
DAY 2 31 g net carbs 2,402 calories	Asparagus and Gruyère Quiche (1 slice) (page 39) Coffee with 2 tablespoons (30 ml) of cream	Chicken Burrito Bowls with Lime Crema (page 70)	Crab Cakes with Spinach and Artichokes (page 101) Cheesy Bread Sticks (2 sticks) (page 191) Almond Panna Cotta (page 239)	Meat and Cheese Rolls (Roast Beef and Pepper Jack Rolls; page 208) Cheddar Zucchini Crisps (2 servings) (page 192)
DAY 3 28 g net carbs 2,415 calories	Coconut and Almond Granola (page 27) with 1 cup (240 ml) of unsweet-ened almond milk Coffee with 2 tablespoons (30 ml) of cream	Spicy Chicken and Greens (page 114) Mini Chai-Spiced Cheesecake (page 228)	Breaded Meatballs with Pesto Noodles (page 83) Garlic-Herb Bread (page 161)	Almond Fat Bomb Fudge (page 221)

(continued)

Shelly's 3-Day Meal Plan

	BREAKFAST	LUNCH	DINNER	SNACKS
DAY 1 23 g net carbs 2,051 calories	Fasting	Spiced Beef Koftas with Tahini Dipping Sauce (page 110) Garlic-Herb Bread (page 161)	Vietnamese Lemongrass Pork Noodle Bowl (page 106) Chocolate Crepes Two Ways (Kumquat Crepes; page 23)	Cinnamon-Flax Almond Muffin (page 28)
DAY 2 25 g net carbs 2,026 calories	Fasting	Cheesy Dairy-Free Tofu Scramble (page 40) Hazelnut Truffle Fat Bombs (2 truffles) (page 218) Coconut Matcha Latte (page 48)	Monterey Chicken (page 86) Radish Au Gratin (page 165) Mini Chai-Spiced Cheesecake (page 228)	Curried Deviled Eggs (2 servings) (page 199) Cinnamon-Flax Almond Muffin (page 28) with 1 tablespoon (14 g) butter
DAY 3 24 g net carbs 2,074 calories	Fasting	Steak Arugula Salad (page 136) Cream of Cauliflower Soup (page 148)	Spicy Korean Short Ribs with Crispy Cabbage (page 93) Strawberry, Lime and Basil Granita (page 236)	Meat and Cheese Rolls (Rotisserie Chicken and Sharp Cheddar; 3 servings; page 208) Pine Nut Biscotti (page 231)

Q&A with Anna Dornier, NASM-CPT and Keto Coach

I keep messing up. How can I make it easier to stay keto?

It's okay to mess up, especially at the very beginning of your keto journey, because it is a *journey*. This is not just another diet to try. It is a lifestyle change. If you have the mindset that this is going to be a long-term lifestyle for you, then each meal and each day is a step toward progress.

Take it one meal at a time. For example, at a restaurant —a place where it's easy to "mess up"—look for meals that have ample veggies and have a fattier cut of protein (i.e., chicken thighs instead of chicken breast or rib eye instead of sirloin steak). Add more fats in the form of a salad dressing or extra butter on your veggies, or have a fat bomb ready for dessert at home.

How long will it be until I see results/progress/get into ketosis?

Everyone is different, but in general, when you are consistent with your macronutrient ratios, you can get into ketosis within 3 days to 3 weeks. There are many factors that can affect how quickly you can get into ketosis: how sensitive you are to carbs (i.e., insulin resistant, pre-diabetic or diabetic), how active you are, how much sleep you're getting and how stressed you are . . . just to name a few.

I also suggest taking "before" pictures and measurements of various body parts that you want to track, such as the area around your belly button, hips and thighs, for instance. This way, you'll have ways other than weight to measure your progress. Remember, you want to protect muscle—which is important to overall health—so you may not see a change on the scale. As the old saying goes, a picture is worth a thousand words.

What if other people in my family aren't eating keto?

Not everyone will join you in your journey, and that's okay. My best advice is to stay consistent and be your own best advocate for keto. Once you start seeing results and your family sees the positive changes you are making—not only in your physical appearance, but also with your improved mood and increased energy—they might join you later in your journey. If you are the cook in the family, you can always make your main dish keto and give the rest of your family a carb option as a side dish. A pot of rice or noodles can be a quick addition.

I miss (or crave) bread/fruit/sugar/etc. What should I do?

This is very normal, especially at the very beginning of your journey. Your body was accustomed to using carbs for energy and it hasn't yet developed the proper metabolic machinery to turn fats into ketones for fuel. You are also fighting most of the habits that you may have developed around carbs, like snacking on high-carb foods at night or when you're stressed. It does get better. Give yourself a lot of grace during this process and understand that change is not going to happen overnight. Make sure that you drink plenty of water and electrolytes to stay hydrated. It's common to mistake dehydration for hunger or cravings.

Do I have to eat if I'm not hungry?

When you're in ketosis, your blood sugar is stable and your body has access to your stored body fat for energy, which means you may be at less risk for losing muscle. Many people who eat keto also practice some form of intermittent fasting, which means restricting eating to only certain hours of the day.

Do I have to fast?

No, you don't have to fast. But if you do feel that fasting fits your lifestyle better and you can skip meals easily because of your reduced appetite, then you may find an intermittent fasting schedule that suits your life, your needs and your goals.

Can I eat keto even if I don't cook?

The short answer is "yes," but we've found that some basic cooking skills are necessary for any healthy lifestyle change. Eating out can become expensive and you do not have much control over the quality of ingredients or how foods are prepared. I suggest starting with simple recipes from this cookbook, and then working your way up to more elaborate ones as you get more comfortable with this way of eating and your cooking skills develop. You might find that you actually enjoy cooking delicious keto meals for yourself and your family!

Iced Almond Matcha Latte (page 49)

Beauty Matcha Latte (page 49)

Coconut Matcha Latte (page 48)

morning food

Starting your keto day right is essential to keeping on track, but it can be difficult to find substitutes for what is often the most carb-laden meal in the standard American diet. Don't despair! If you miss traditional pancakes or crepes, the fluffy Blueberry-Lemon Pancakes (page 18) or luxurious Chocolate Crepes Two Ways (page 21) will satisfy your cravings. If you prefer a savory egg-based breakfast, try the rich Bacon, Cheese and Watercress Omelettes (page 36) or the Egg and Spicy Rice Brunch Bowl (page 35). That said, we know it is easy to get tired of eggs every day—the Cheesy Dairy-Free Tofu Scramble (page 40) and Raspberry, Radish and Goat Cheese Breakfast Salad (page 43) make nice alternatives.

Crunched for time? We've included several make-ahead recipes. Coconut and Almond Granola (page 27) is a family-friendly quick breakfast paired with your favorite plant-based milk, and Mini Mean Green Quiches (page 31) store well for 5 days in the refrigerator. Raspberry Cheesecake Breakfast Pots (page 24) can be made ahead and portioned in small jars for a grab-and-go breakfast or snack.

We have also included several recipes for beverages that are a dream at breakfast or throughout the day. Vanilla Rooibos Tea with Cream Froth (page 47) is a quick way to add extra fats first thing in the morning, and our Very Berry Tea (page 51) and Blackberry Smoothie (page 44) can satisfy fruit cravings any time of day.

easy keto breakfasts

Don't get stuck in a breakfast rut—other "non-breakfast" recipes throughout this cookbook work well for quick morning food. That said, "dinner food" also works for breakfast; sometimes a bowl of leftovers or a slice of cold low-carb pizza can hit the spot.

Fried Egg Sandwich made with Buttermilk Biscuits (page 158) and Herby Italian Garlic-Parm Compound Butter (page 184)

Mini Chai-Spiced Cheesecakes (page 228)

Scrambled Eggs with Garlic-Herb Bread (page 161)

Kimchi Fried Cauli-Rice (page 166) topped with a fried egg

Thai Omelette (page 62)

Almond Panna Cotta (page 239) topped with fresh berries

Cucumber, Egg and Lox Bites (page 211)

Blueberry-Lemon Pancakes

2 g net carbs

30 Minutes or Less   Vegetarian

These pancakes have the fluffy texture and nutty flavor of a traditional whole wheat pancake but are made with flaxseed and almonds instead of flour. They brown quickly, so keep an eye on the pan when cooking. These make for a winning family breakfast with a pat of butter and a drizzle of keto maple-flavored syrup.

 Prep time: 8 minutes

 Cook time: 10 minutes

 Makes 8 pancakes

Add the almond flour, flaxseed, erythritol, 1 tablespoon (14 g) of the butter, baking soda, lemon juice, lemon zest, almond butter, vanilla and salt to a food processor. Blend well to combine.

Add the eggs and blend again until you have a smooth and thick, yet pourable, batter. Pour the batter into a bowl and let it stand for 10 minutes.

Add the blueberries to the batter and stir through.

Melt a teaspoon of butter in a large skillet over medium heat. When the butter has melted, add a little less than ¼ cup (60 ml) of the batter to the hot skillet, pouring into a rough pancake shape, then repeat with a second portion of batter. Cook for 45 seconds to 1 minute or until firm and brown on the underside and bubbles appear on the surface. Flip the pancakes and cook for another 45 seconds or until golden brown all over and cooked through. Repeat with the remaining batter, greasing the pan with extra butter between batches as needed. You should get eight pancakes from the mixture.

Keep the pancakes warm and serve with your favorite keto toppings.

¾ cup (70 g) almond flour

⅓ cup (35 g) ground flaxseed

1 tbsp (12 g) erythritol

2 tbsp (28 g) butter, divided

½ tsp baking soda

1 tsp lemon juice

1 tsp lemon zest

1 tbsp (15 g) almond butter

1 tsp vanilla extract

⅛ tsp salt

3 medium eggs

⅓ cup (50 g) blueberries

Weight: 1.4 oz (40 g) per pancake

Net Carbs
2 g

Protein
5 g

Fat
13 g

153 Calories

 6 g total carbs

 3 g fiber

Keto Coach Says:

You can make these pancakes ahead of time and store them in the freezer. This makes it convenient during busy weekday mornings to have a ready-made breakfast. Separate the pancakes with parchment paper and store in a plastic resealable bag or container. Throw them in the toaster oven for 5 minutes at 350°F (175°C) to heat them up. Enjoy!

Chocolate Crepes Two Ways

3 g net carbs

In coming up with this recipe, we tried to find a way to make classic keto crepes taste less "egg-y," a common complaint. The dark cocoa powder does the trick and the crepes work well with any sweet topping. We include xanthan gum to help hold the crepes together. While it is possible to leave it out, if you do, you will need to take additional care when flipping the crepes. We've provided two flavor variations for tasty fillings—make sure to try them both!

Blend the cream cheese, eggs, coconut flour, powdered erythritol, xanthan gum and cocoa powder in a medium bowl with a stick blender until fully combined. The batter should be slightly thicker than heavy cream—add up to 1 tablespoon (15 ml) of water if the batter is too thick to pour.

Preheat a 6-inch (15-cm) nonstick pan over medium-high heat. Using a pastry brush, swipe a small amount of melted butter over the hot pan.

Add ¼ cup (60 ml) of the batter into the center of the hot pan. Swirl the pan three to four times to move the batter around in a circle, being sure to move the batter around to cover any holes. Allow the crepe to cook, turning the heat down slightly if you see any smoking. Wait until the crepe starts to turn brown on the edges before using a spatula to start loosening the edges. If the crepe is ready to flip, you should be able to get the spatula under the very center of the crepe, lift it and flip it over. It should be very easy. If it is not ready to be flipped, the spatula will rip the crepe. If this happens, push the crepe back together and allow it to cook for a few more seconds. Repeat with the remaining batter. The batter should yield about eight crepes, depending on thickness.

If you want to make the crepes ahead of time, you can place them in a stack and wrap with plastic wrap before freezing or refrigerating. The crepes will keep for 5 days in the refrigerator and up to 2 months in the freezer.

4 oz (113 g) cream cheese, softened

4 eggs

2 tsp (5 g) coconut flour

2 tsp (8 g) powdered erythritol (such as Swerve confectioners')

⅛ tsp xanthan gum

1 tbsp (5 g) dark cocoa powder

1 tbsp (14 g) butter, melted

Did You Know?

There are many different brands of erythritol available. We used the Swerve brand of both powdered and granulated sweetener, which includes a prebiotic and oligosaccharides blend and is slightly sweeter than straight erythritol, as well as pure granulated erythritol. We encourage you to experiment and find what works best for you. If you do substitute other sweeteners in the recipes in this book, the texture and flavor might change. These recipes have been tested with sweeteners that are formulated 1:1 to replace sugar, so adjust for sweetness accordingly.

(continued)

Vegetarian

Prep time:
15 minutes

Cook time:
25 minutes

Serves: 4
(2 crepes per serving)

Weight: 2.6 oz (75 g) per serving

Net Carbs
 3 g

Protein
 8 g

Fat
18 g

211 Calories

5 g total carbs

1 g fiber

Strawberry Chantilly Crepes

6 g net carbs

Wash and quarter the strawberries. Mix in 1 teaspoon of erythritol and a pinch of salt. Set aside.

Whip the heavy cream and the remaining teaspoon of erythritol together with a whisk until medium peaks form. Add the vanilla and whisk to combine.

Place 1 tablespoon (15 g) of the quartered sweetened strawberries and 1 tablespoon (15 ml) of the sweetened whipped cream into the middle of a chocolate crepe. Fold the crepe in half once and then fold it in half again to form a triangle. Repeat with the remaining crepes. Serve immediately.

1 cup (144 g) strawberries

2 tsp (8 g) powdered erythritol, divided

⅛ tsp kosher salt

½ cup (120 ml) heavy cream

½ tsp vanilla

1 batch cooked Chocolate Crepes (page 21)

Vegetarian | 6+ Grams Net Carbs

 Prep time: 15 minutes

 Cook time: 25 minutes

 Serves: 4 (2 crepes per serving)

Weight: 5.5 oz (156 g) per serving

Net Carbs
6 g

Protein
10 g

Fat
29 g

326 Calories

 10 g total carbs

 1 g fiber

Kumquat Crepes

5 g net carbs

Wash and thinly slice the kumquats, removing any seeds but keeping the peel. Toss with the cinnamon and 1 teaspoon of erythritol. Set aside.

Whip the heavy cream and the remaining teaspoon of erythritol with a whisk until medium peaks form.

Place 1 heaping teaspoon of the kumquat mixture and 1 tablespoon (15 ml) of the sweetened whipped cream into the middle of a chocolate crepe. Fold the crepe in half once and then fold it in half again to form a triangle. Repeat with the remaining crepes.

½ cup (73 g) kumquats

¼ tsp cinnamon

2 tsp (8 g) powdered erythritol, divided

½ cup (120 ml) heavy cream

1 batch cooked Chocolate Crepes (page 21)

Did You Know?

Kumquats, a small relative of tangerines and other citrus fruits, should be eaten whole. Their peel is naturally sweet, contrasting with their pucker-inducing flesh. They're packed with fiber and vitamin C, and, in small portions, are a keto-friendly fruit.

Vegetarian

Prep time:
15 minutes

Cook time:
25 minutes

Serves: 4
(2 crepes per serving)

Weight: 4.8 oz (136 g) per serving

Net Carbs
 5 g

Protein
10 g

Fat
29 g

326
Calories

 10 g total carbs

 2 g fiber

Raspberry Cheesecake Breakfast Pots

3 g net carbs

These sweet and creamy cheesecake parfaits are loaded with rich Greek yogurt, cream cheese, juicy raspberries and an almond crumble. These are a decadent make-ahead breakfast option, and even work as a post-dinner treat! If fresh raspberries are out of season, frozen raspberries work just as well.

To prepare the crumble, add the almond flour, powdered erythritol and salt to a mixing bowl and stir to combine. Melt the coconut oil over low heat on the stovetop or in a microwave for 20 to 30 seconds, then add it to the bowl. Stir the coconut oil into the dry ingredients well to coat the almond flour and achieve a sandy, crumbly texture. Place the bowl in the refrigerator while you prepare the remaining ingredients.

For the cheesecake layer, add the cream cheese and powdered erythritol to a small mixing bowl and mash together with a spoon. Then, add the yogurt and vanilla and stir until well combined.

Place the raspberries in a small bowl and gently crush them with a fork.

In the bottom of four ramekins or serving glasses, first place a layer of the crumble, then the cream cheese mixture, then the crushed raspberries. Repeat the layers again, so that you will get a mix of crumble, raspberry and cheesecake with each bite. Refrigerate for at least 2 hours, or until ready to serve.

Crumble

6 tbsp (40 g) almond flour

2 tsp (8 g) powdered erythritol or low-carb sweetener of choice

¼ tsp salt

1 tbsp (14 g) coconut oil

Cheesecake Layer

¼ cup (60 g) cream cheese, softened

2 tbsp (24 g) powdered erythritol or low-carb sweetener of choice

¼ cup (62 g) full-fat Greek yogurt, plain

1 tsp vanilla extract

Topping

⅔ cup (82 g) fresh raspberries

Vegetarian

Prep time:
10 minutes

Cook time:
2 minutes + at least
120 minutes chill time

Serves: 4

Weight: 2.75 oz (78 g) per serving

Net Carbs
 3 g

Protein
5 g

Fat
13 g

162
Calories

14 g total carbs

2 g fiber

Coconut and Almond Granola

5 g net carbs

This crisp, golden granola is a great way to start the day. It is packed with healthy fats from coconut, almonds and chia seeds. Using chopped and sliced almonds and flaked and shredded coconut gives the granola a satisfying texture. It is perfect served with your favorite plant-based milk.

This recipe makes four portions but it can easily be doubled. Stored in an airtight container, it can provide you an entire week of breakfasts.

Preheat the oven to 275°F (140°C), and line a shallow baking pan with parchment paper.

Roughly chop the whole almonds with a large, sharp knife. There should be some larger and some smaller pieces—the variety improves the texture of the granola. Place the chopped almonds in a large mixing bowl along with the sliced almonds, flaked coconut, shredded coconut and chia seeds. Stir well to combine.

Melt the coconut oil over low heat on the stovetop or in a microwave for 20 to 30 seconds, then add it to the nut mixture along with the ground ginger, vanilla, erythritol and salt. Stir well, coating the nuts, coconut and seeds in the flavorings and oil.

Spread the granola in an even layer across the parchment-lined baking pan and bake for 25 minutes until crisp and golden brown, stirring halfway through the baking time. Allow the granola to cool completely, then transfer to an airtight container to store.

½ cup (72 g) whole almonds
½ cup (54 g) sliced almonds
½ cup (40 g) flaked coconut
½ cup (40 g) shredded coconut
1 tbsp (10 g) chia seeds
1 tbsp (14 g) coconut oil
1½ tsp (3 g) ground ginger
1 tsp vanilla extract
1 tbsp (12 g) erythritol
⅛ tsp sea salt

Dairy Free   Vegetarian

 Prep time:
10 minutes

Cook time:
25 minutes

Serves: 4

Weight: 2 oz (57 g) per serving

Net Carbs
 5 g

Protein
 8 g

Fat
32 g

351
Calories

16 g total carbs

8 g fiber

Cinnamon-Flax Almond Muffins

3 g net carbs

These family-friendly Cinnamon-Flax Almond Muffins are the perfect on-the-go breakfast. The soft, moist muffin interiors taste a little bit like cornbread with a delicious flaxseed-cinnamon streusel.

Preheat the oven to 350°F (175°C). Line a muffin tin with twelve liners. Add the almond flour, powdered erythritol, baking powder and salt to a medium bowl and whisk to combine.

Add the eggs, coconut oil (melted or solid), vanilla and almond milk to the bowl with the dry ingredients. Mix the wet ingredients into the dry with a spatula to combine.

To make the streusel, stir together the flaxseed, coconut oil, powdered erythritol and cinnamon.

Using a cookie scoop or two spoons, scoop 12 even scoops of the muffin batter into the muffin liners and top with 2 teaspoons (8 g) of streusel topping per muffin.

Bake for 20 to 22 minutes until the muffins are golden and cooked through. Allow the muffins to cool before serving.

Muffins

3 cups (290 g) almond flour

½ cup (96 g) powdered erythritol (Swerve confectioners' preferred)

1½ tsp (8 g) baking powder

¼ tsp kosher salt

3 large eggs

⅓ cup (72 g) coconut oil

½ tsp vanilla extract

⅓ cup (80 ml) unsweetened almond milk

Streusel Topping

½ cup (50 g) ground flaxseed

2 tbsp (28 g) coconut oil

2 tbsp (24 g) powdered erythritol (Swerve confectioners' preferred)

1 tsp cinnamon

 Dairy Free
 Vegetarian

 Prep time: 15 minutes

 Cook time: 22 minutes

 Makes 12 muffins

Weight: 2 oz (57 g) per muffin

Net Carbs
3 g

Protein
8 g

Fat
25 g

 285 Calories

 15 g total carbs

 5 g fiber

Mini Mean Green Quiches

2 g net carbs

These tiny veggie-packed quiches with almond crusts are a convenient grab-and-go breakfast or make-ahead snack. Cooking the quiches in muffin cups makes portioning easy. One is a perfect-sized snack, and two to three make a great breakfast. Layer the quiches in an airtight container and store in the refrigerator for up to 5 days.

Preheat the oven to 350°F (175°C). Line a muffin tin with twelve silicone liners. (Paper liners will work, but silicone is a better choice to prevent any sticking.)

Mix the almond flour with the olive oil and the salt. Divide the mixture between the twelve cups and press it down with the back of a spoon. Bake for 10 minutes. Remove the muffin tin from the oven and allow the crusts to cool slightly in the tin.

Whisk together the salt and eggs, then add the spinach, parsley and broccoli.

Divide the mixture between the twelve muffin cups on top of the almond crust.

Top each cup with shredded cheese and bake again for 18 to 22 minutes, until the egg is puffed and cooked through.

Crust

1 cup (96 g) almond flour

4 tsp (20 ml) olive oil

⅛ tsp kosher salt

Filling

¼ tsp kosher salt

10 large eggs

½ cup (12 g) baby spinach

1 tbsp (4 g) chopped parsley

½ cup (46 g) chopped broccoli florets

½ cup (56 g) shredded cheddar cheese

Vegetarian

Prep time:
15 minutes

Cook time:
32 minutes

Makes 12 mini quiches

Weight: 2 oz (57 g) per mini quiche

Net Carbs
2 g

Protein
8 g

Fat
12 g

152
Calories

3 g total carbs

1 g fiber

Sunny-Side Up Aleppo Eggs

2 g net carbs

This dish makes a filling breakfast or brunch. Healthy and hearty kale and zucchini are roasted with sunny-side up eggs sprinkled with Aleppo chili pepper and salt. We start the vegetables first and then add the eggs, so that everything will be completed at the same time. If you like your eggs firm, add a few extra minutes in the oven. Serve with Garlic-Herb Bread (page 161) and your favorite Compound Butter (page 183).

Preheat the oven to 425°F (220°C). Wash and slice the zucchini lengthwise into quarters and then into small slices about ½ inch (1 cm) thick. For easy clean-up, line a rimmed baking sheet with parchment paper.

Wash and strip the kale leaves from the stem if the stem is particularly thick. Chop into 1-inch (2.5-cm) pieces. Place the zucchini and kale in a medium bowl and toss with the olive oil and salt.

Place the vegetables onto the rimmed baking sheet in a single layer. Bake for 10 minutes, until the vegetables are starting to soften and brown.

Remove the baking sheet pan from the oven and crack the eggs over the top of the vegetables. Season the eggs with kosher salt and the Aleppo pepper. Bake for 8 to 10 minutes, until the whites of the eggs are opaque and the yolks are starting to set. Serve hot.

Vegetables

1 medium zucchini

2½ cups (168 g) dinosaur/lacinato kale

1½ tbsp (22 ml) extra-virgin olive oil

¼ tsp kosher salt

Eggs

4 large raw eggs

⅛ tsp kosher salt

⅛ tsp Aleppo chili pepper

Dairy Free 30 Minutes or Less

Vegetarian Paleo

Prep time:
10 minutes

Cook time:
20 minutes

Serves: 4

Weight: 4.8 oz (137 g) per serving

Net Carbs
2 g

Protein
7 g

Fat
11 g

134
Calories

3 g total carbs

1 g fiber

Egg and Spicy Rice Brunch Bowl

5 g net carbs

Dairy Free   **30 Minutes or Less**

Vegetarian   **Paleo**

This colorful bowl is layered with spiced cauliflower rice, creamy avocado and a simple fresh-made salsa and is topped with a fried egg. If you substitute a premade salsa, look for one with 1 gram or fewer of carbohydrates per serving. This makes a flavorful meat-free brunch, breakfast or even lunch. Feel free to adjust the seasonings if you prefer more or less heat. A tablespoon (12 g) of sour cream or a drizzle of hot sauce would be a great addition.

Prep time: 8 minutes

Cook time: 8 minutes

Serves: 4

To prepare the salsa, finely dice the tomatoes and roughly chop the cilantro. Add both to a small bowl, then stir in the lime juice, olive oil, salt and pepper to combine; set aside.

To prepare the spicy rice, add the cauliflower rice, paprika, oregano, lime zest, cumin, chili powder, vegetable stock, garlic powder and salt to a small pan over medium heat and stir well to combine. Simmer for 7 to 8 minutes, until the rice is hot throughout and all the stock has been absorbed.

While the rice is cooking, heat the olive oil in a skillet over medium heat. Crack the eggs into the skillet and fry to your preference. Thinly slice the avocado and roughly chop the lettuce. Divide between two serving bowls, then add the spicy rice and salsa. Top each bowl with a fried egg. Season with more salt and pepper if desired and scatter with dried chili flakes to serve.

Salsa

8 cherry tomatoes

2 tbsp (2 g) fresh cilantro

2 tsp (10 ml) lime juice

2 tsp (10 ml) olive oil

⅛ tsp salt

⅛ tsp black pepper

Spicy Rice

2½ cups (285 g) fresh or frozen cauliflower rice

2 tsp (5 g) smoked paprika

2 tsp (2 g) dried oregano

1 tsp lime zest

1 tsp ground cumin

2 tsp (5 g) chili powder

½ cup (120 ml) vegetable stock

½ tsp garlic powder

½ tsp salt

Toppings

1½ tbsp (22 ml) olive oil

4 eggs

1 medium avocado

1 cup (60 g) lettuce

1 tsp dried chili flakes

Weight: 5 oz (142 g) per serving

Net Carbs
 5 g

Protein
9 g

Fat
19 g

238 Calories

 11 g total carbs

 6 g fiber

Bacon, Cheese and Watercress Omelettes

4 g net carbs

These simple but flavorful omelettes are rich with an oozy layer of melted cheddar cheese, peppery watercress and crisp bacon. This makes a hearty breakfast or brunch option—perfect for keeping you satiated until lunch. A few berries make a nice side.

Melt ½ tablespoon (7 g) of butter in a 6-inch (15-cm) skillet over medium heat. Roughly dice the bacon, add it to the skillet and cook until crisp and golden, 3 to 4 minutes. Remove the bacon with a slotted spoon and set aside, keeping warm.

While the bacon is cooking, add the eggs, salt and pepper to a mixing bowl and beat to combine.

Melt half of the remaining butter in the skillet used to cook the bacon. Add half of the shallot slices and sweat them over low heat for 1 or 2 minutes to allow them to soften. Pour half of the beaten egg onto the shallots and increase the heat to medium.

Leave the egg to cook for 1 minute, untouched, then use a spatula to gently ease the cooked edges of the omelette away from the sides of the skillet, allowing any uncooked liquid to flow around the edges. Once the omelette is just cooked through, sprinkle half of the cheese over one side of the omelette and let it melt for a moment.

Remove the skillet from the heat and scatter the watercress over the cheese. Sprinkle the bacon over the watercress.

Repeat with the remaining butter, shallots, egg, watercress and bacon for the second omelette. Serve as is or with a light salad.

1 tbsp (14 g) unsalted butter, divided

4 slices bacon

6 medium eggs

⅛ tsp sea salt

⅛ tsp black pepper

¼ large shallot, thinly sliced

½ cup (56 g) grated cheddar cheese

½ cup (20 g) watercress, thick stems discarded

Prep time: 8 minutes

Cook time: 10 minutes

Serves: 2

Weight: 5.5 oz (156 g) per serving

Net Carbs
 4 g

Protein
29 g

Fat
35 g

451 Calories

4 g total carbs

<1 g fiber

Asparagus and Gruyère Quiche

4 g net carbs

This is a great make-ahead breakfast that is easy to portion and reheats well. Eat a slice for breakfast or prepare with a tossed salad dressed with Herbs de Provence Apple Cider Vinaigrette (page 144) to make a complete meal for lunch. We recommend using a tart pan with a solid bottom so that the filling will not leak. If you don't mind a more rustic appearance, a 9.5-inch (24-cm) pie pan works just as well. Other cheeses, like Jarlsberg, Swiss or Gouda, can be substituted for the Gruyère.

Preheat the oven to 350°F (175°C). In a medium mixing bowl, combine the almond flour, melted butter and kosher salt. Mix well to make a dough.

Place the dough in the bottom of an 11-inch (28-cm) tart pan (or a 9.5-inch [24-cm] pie pan) and press the dough evenly on the bottom and up the sides of the pan. Bake the crust for 12 minutes.

Preheat a frying pan over medium heat, then add the avocado oil and asparagus. Gently cook until some of the rawness is cooked off, about 1 minute. Add a pinch of salt to the asparagus and stir. Turn off the heat.

In a medium mixing bowl (you can use the same one that you used for the dough), combine the eggs, water, cream and ½ teaspoon kosher salt. Beat until everything is well mixed.

Place the asparagus on the bottom of the tart, then cover with the grated Gruyère.

Carefully pour the egg mixture over the asparagus and cheese and bake the quiche for 40 minutes, or until just set and lightly browned. Allow the quiche to cool for 5 minutes before serving. Refrigerate for up to 4 days.

Dough

2 cups (190 g) almond flour

5 tbsp (70 g) butter, melted

⅛ tsp kosher salt

Quiche

1 tsp avocado oil

2¼ cups (300 g) asparagus, ½-inch (13-mm) pieces

½ tsp + a pinch of kosher salt, divided

4 eggs

¾ cup (180 ml) water

¾ cup (180 ml) cream

1 cup (112 g) grated Gruyère cheese

Keto Coach Says:

Asparagus contains oligofructose, which our gut bacteria loves to eat! These are also called prebiotics—food for our gut bacteria. Other vegetables that have a good amount of oligofructose are onions, leeks and Jerusalem artichokes.

Vegetarian

Prep time: 20 minutes

Cook time: 60 minutes

Serves: 8

Weight: 4 oz (113 g) per serving

Net Carbs
4 g

Protein
15 g

Fat
37 g

408 Calories

8 g total carbs

4 g fiber

Cheesy Dairy-Free Tofu Scramble

3 g net carbs

Cheesy with no dairy! This simple tofu scramble is a great breakfast alternative to eggs, rich with plant-based protein and a cheesy tang from nutritional yeast. This is a satisfying breakfast, or even lunch, option served with keto toast or tucked into Buttermilk Biscuits (page 158), if you do dairy.

Wrap the tofu in a clean tea towel or paper towels. Place a heavy weighted item on top of the tofu (or press gently with the palm of your hand) to squeeze any excess liquid from the tofu.

Very roughly crumble the tofu into a mixing bowl, so it resembles chunks of scrambled eggs. Add the turmeric, nutritional yeast, lemon juice, salt and pepper. Stir together gently to combine. Add the almond milk and gently stir into the tofu.

Melt the coconut oil in a skillet over medium heat. Add the tofu and allow to cook and brown for 3 to 4 minutes, then gently flip the tofu over and cook until the tofu is lightly golden, about 2 to 3 additional minutes.

Add the spinach to the skillet. Stir gently into the tofu and allow to cook until the spinach is just wilted and the tofu is hot throughout and golden.

Top the avocado with the scrambled tofu and scatter with fresh parsley to serve.

18 oz (510 g) extra-firm tofu

½ tsp ground turmeric

3 tbsp (15 g) nutritional yeast

1 tsp lemon juice

¼ tsp sea salt

⅛ tsp black pepper

2 tbsp (30 ml) unsweetened almond milk

1 tbsp (14 g) coconut oil

2 cups (60 g) baby spinach

2 avocados, sliced into thin wedges

2 tbsp (8 g) fresh parsley

30 Minutes or Less | Vegetarian | Dairy Free

 Prep time: 6 minutes

 Cook time: 8 minutes

 Serves: 4

Weight: 1.8 oz (50 g) per serving

Net Carbs
3 g

Protein
16 g

Fat
21 g

272 Calories

 10 g total carbs

 6 g fiber

Raspberry, Radish and Goat Cheese Breakfast Salad

3 g net carbs

This delicious sweet and tangy salad is the perfect keto breakfast or brunch alternative to typical breakfast meats and egg-based dishes. Packed with sweet raspberries, crisp radishes, aromatic mint, tangy goat cheese and crunchy seeds, this is a refreshing way to start the day, keeping you satiated until lunch. If you have access to watercress, it makes a great substitution for the arugula.

Add the arugula, avocado, radishes and mint to a large serving bowl. Toss to combine.

Crumble the goat cheese into bite-size chunks and scatter over the salad. Season everything with salt and pepper and toss to combine.

Whisk together the oil and lemon juice and drizzle over the salad.

Scatter with the seeds and raspberries to serve.

4 cups (80 g) arugula

1 medium avocado, thinly sliced

8 medium radishes, thinly sliced

3 tbsp (17 g) fresh mint, roughly chopped

3.5 oz (100 g) goat cheese

½ tsp salt

⅛ tsp black pepper

2 tbsp (30 ml) olive oil

1 tbsp (15 ml) lemon juice

1 tbsp (8 g) pumpkin seeds

1 tbsp (8 g) sunflower seeds

40 raspberries

 30 Minutes or Less   Vegetarian

 Prep time:
10 minutes

 Cook time:
0 minutes

Serves: 4

Weight: 4.3 oz (122 g) per serving

Net Carbs
3 g

Protein
7 g

Fat
19 g

222 Calories

 7 g total carbs

 4 g fiber

Blackberry Smoothie

4 g net carbs

If you miss fruit, this is a good way to satisfy that craving while adding some extra fats into your day. Sip it for breakfast or a mid-morning pick-me-up. If you decide to add the optional stevia, the fresh mint and lime help balance the herbal stevia flavor.

Add the blackberries, almond milk, avocado, lime juice, vanilla, peppermint leaves and stevia (if using) to a blender and mix until creamy. You can also use a handheld immersion blender. Garnish with a slice of lime, if desired.

10 blackberries (fresh or frozen)

½ cup (120 ml) unsweetened almond milk

½ medium avocado

1 tsp fresh lime juice

¼ tsp vanilla extract

3–4 fresh peppermint or spearmint leaves

3 drops liquid stevia (optional)

Small slice of lime, for garnish (optional)

Keto Coach Says:

Research suggests that fasting is the best way to induce autophagy. Autophagy is our body's way to cleanse its cells by breaking down and recycling cellular components. Our body does this to get rid of dead cells or make new ones. New tissues and cells are built to replace those that were destroyed. But it only works if the old parts are discarded first. Accumulation of older cell components can lead to accelerated aging and cancer, so fasting may be a good way to reduce the risk of both.

Dairy Free **30 Minutes or Less**

Vegetarian **Paleo**

Prep time:
3 minutes

Cook time:
0 minutes

Serves: 1

Weight: 8.5 oz (241 g)

Net Carbs
4 g

Protein
3 g

Fat
12 g

155
Calories

12 g total carbs

8 g fiber

Vanilla Rooibos Tea with Cream Froth

2 g net carbs

The recipe prepared below is for cold tea, but this is also delicious hot. The sweet vanilla rooibos pairs perfectly with lightly sweetened and slightly salty cream froth. The cream topping is also delicious on hot coffee!

Steep the vanilla rooibos tea in the boiling water for 5 to 6 minutes. If making iced tea, chill in the refrigerator for at least 15 minutes, until cold. Remove the tea bag.

Add the cream to a milk frother along with the stevia and pinch of salt. Froth the cream until thick and no longer runny. If you do not have a milk frother, you can use a Mason jar fitted with a lid and shake the cream until thick.

Pour the tea into a glass filled with ice and top with the cream froth. If serving hot, skip the ice and pour the cream froth directly onto the hot tea.

1 vanilla rooibos tea bag

⅔ cup (160 ml) boiling water

¼ cup (60 ml) heavy cream

3–4 drops liquid stevia

Pinch of kosher salt

1 cup (110 g) ice cubes

Keto Coach Says:

Stevia is an intensely sweet-tasting plant that has been used to sweeten beverages and make tea since the sixteenth century. It is also a relevant source of natural phenolic compounds, which have antioxidant and antimicrobial properties.

30 Minutes or Less   Vegetarian

 Prep time: 5 minutes

 Cook time: 6 minutes + 15 minutes chill time for iced tea

Serves: 1

Weight: 8.5 oz (241 g)

Net Carbs
2 g

Protein
2 g

Fat
21 g

202 Calories

 2 g total carbs

 0 g fiber

Coconut Matcha Latte Three Ways

3 g net carbs

Matcha is full of beneficial antioxidants and is a great energy booster that is more gentle than a cup of coffee. This matcha latte is lightened with frothed full-fat coconut milk. If you are using a can of coconut milk that has solidified, running it under hot water and shaking before opening the can will emulsify the coconut fat. Unsweetened almond milk makes a lighter, refreshing version that is delicious when iced. The collagen peptides in the Beauty Matcha Latte (page 49) version are a popular supplement for skin health.

Heat and froth the coconut milk in a milk frother. If you don't have a milk frother, heat the milk and pour it into a jar with a lid, then give it several shakes to create foam.

In a small bowl, whisk together 1 ounce (30 ml) of the water and the matcha until combined and all visible lumps are dissolved. Add the remaining boiling water and whisk again. Pour the tea into a mug. Top with the frothed coconut milk and serve immediately.

* See image on page 16.

(continued)

¼ cup (60 ml) full-fat coconut milk

3 oz (90 ml) boiling water, divided

1 tsp matcha powder

Dairy Free   30 Minutes or Less

Vegetarian   Paleo

 Prep time: 7 minutes

 Cook time: 0 minutes

 Serves: 1

Weight: 4.6 oz (130 g)

Net Carbs
3 g

Protein
1 g

Fat
13 g

126 Calories

 4 g total carbs

 1 g fiber

Iced Almond Matcha Latte

1 g net carbs

Add the almond milk and matcha powder to a blender cup and blend with a stick blender until smooth. Pour the mixture over the ice.

* See image on page 16.

1¼ cups (300 ml) unsweetened vanilla almond milk or milk of choice

1 tsp matcha powder

1¾ cup (194 g) ice cubes

Weight: 10.6 oz (300 g)

Net Carbs
1 g

Protein
2 g

Fat
3 g

41 Calories

2 g total carbs

1 g fiber

Beauty Matcha Latte

1 g net carbs

Add the water, collagen peptides and matcha to a blender cup and blend with a stick blender until frothy. Pour into a mug and serve immediately.

* See image on page 16.

½ cup (120 ml) boiling water

5 tsp (10 g) collagen peptides

1 tsp matcha powder

Weight: 4.6 oz (130 g)

Net Carbs
1 g

Protein
10 g

Fat
0 g

40 Calories

1 g total carbs

1 g fiber

Iced Almond Matcha Latte

Beauty Matcha Latte

Very Berry Tea

1 g net carbs

In this recipe, delicious tart hibiscus tea is steeped and chilled, then poured over ice layered with blueberries, raspberries and blackberries. If you crave fruit for breakfast (or any time) this tea packs a fruity punch without a ton of carbs. This recipe is for one serving, but can be easily doubled or quadrupled for more people.

Combine the tea bag and boiling water in a liquid measuring cup. Allow the tea to steep for 4 to 5 minutes, or as long as you'd like. Remove the tea bag, then add the blueberries, raspberries and blackberries and place the measuring cup in the refrigerator to chill completely, about 15 minutes.

Fill a tall glass with ice and pour the tea over the ice. Serve immediately!

1 hibiscus tea bag

1 cup (240 ml) boiling water

5 blueberries

2 raspberries

2 blackberries

1¼ cups (140 g) ice

Make It New:

Add plain or flavored seltzer water to the tea to add sparkle. Add 1 tablespoon (15 ml) of heavy cream with the seltzer water for a keto Italian soda. Add a cinnamon stick and a slice of orange to the steeping step for an orange-spiced flavor.

Dairy Free

30 Minutes or Less

Vegetarian

Paleo

Prep time:
5 minutes

Cook time:
5 minutes + 15 minutes (chill time)

Serves: 1

Weight: 9 oz (255 g)

Net Carbs
1 g

Protein
<1 g

Fat
<1 g

10
Calories

<1 g total carbs

<1 g fiber

quick & easy

It is seven o'clock on a Wednesday. You just got home from work and the kids are whining, "We're hungry!" Nothing has been defrosted and dreams of frozen pizzas or the quick burger down the street hit the hard reality of going out of ketosis. We've all been there. Why does eating keto take so much time? Meal planning is our aspirational goal, but sometimes we just need quick meals that taste great and hit the spot.

Every recipe in this section, like the luscious Prosciutto, Parmesan and Arugula Tagliatelle (page 65) made with zucchini noodles, the comforting Creamy Shrimp and Wild Rice Risotto (page 57) or the baked Citrus Salmon (page 61), can be made, start to finish, in 30 minutes or less. Put out some nuts for an appetizer and throw together a side salad with your favorite keto dressing (see pages 143, 144 and 147), and a complete dinner is on the table. These recipes also work great for a quick lunch.

Of course life is easier if we plan ahead, but having a few emergency ingredients on hand can save us the pain of a crisis meal. In the freezer, you may want to keep shrimp, salmon, chicken breasts and cauliflower rice on hand. In the refrigerator, have cheese, prosciutto, bacon and low-carb vegetables like zucchini, mushrooms and lettuce ready to use. In the pantry, you may want to have garlic, ginger, chorizo, nuts, citrus, avocados and dried herbs and spices. We've included a Pantry List on page 242 with more ideas.

formulas for fast keto meals

Don't despair if you find yourself in a time crunch and don't have all the ingredients you need for one of the recipes in this chapter. Try this simple formula:

protein + low-carb vegetable + fat = keto dinner.

shrimp + spinach + lemon + butter = lemon butter shrimp on a bed of wilted spinach

egg + cauliflower + olive oil = spanish cauliflower tortilla

nuts + zucchini + cheese = a playful pasta dish

steak + snow peas + sesame oil = stir-fried beef and snow peas

fish + lettuce + sour cream = crunchy lettuce fish tacos

Chorizo and Shrimp Fajitas

6 g net carbs

These juicy chorizo and shrimp fajitas are loaded with aromatic herbs and spices, stuffed with tender low-carb veggies and topped with a zesty guacamole. A crisp lettuce wrap replaces the usual tortilla. These make a flavorful lunch or a quick, simple dinner.

Heat the oil in a large skillet over medium heat and add the chorizo, cooking for 1 minute or so, until lightly browned and starting to release its oils. Add the zucchini, bell pepper, cumin, coriander, paprika, oregano, garlic powder, salt and pepper. Stir well to combine and continue to cook for 3 to 4 minutes until the vegetables soften.

Add the shrimp to the skillet and stir well. Cook for 3 to 4 minutes, or until the shrimp has turned pink and is cooked through.

While the shrimp and chorizo are cooking, add the avocados to a mixing bowl. Add 1 tablespoon (1 g) of the cilantro and the green onions, lime juice and a pinch of salt and pepper. Roughly mash the avocados together with the other ingredients to create a chunky guacamole.

To serve, divide the fajita filling between the lettuce leaves and top with the guacamole, sour cream and remaining cilantro.

Filling

2 tbsp (30 ml) olive oil

3.5 oz (100 g) Spanish chorizo, sliced into 1-inch (3-cm) chunks

1⅓ cups (165 g) zucchini, sliced into 1-inch (3-cm) chunks

1 medium red bell pepper, cored and thinly sliced

1 tsp ground cumin

2 tsp (4 g) ground coriander

2 tsp (5 g) smoked paprika

2 tsp (2 g) dried oregano

1 tsp garlic powder

¼ tsp sea salt

⅛ tsp black pepper

6 oz (170 g) peeled raw jumbo shrimp

Toppings

2 medium avocados, mashed

2 tbsp (2 g) fresh cilantro, roughly chopped, divided

2 small green onions, thinly sliced

2 tsp (10 ml) lime juice

Salt and pepper, to taste

4 large romaine lettuce leaves, washed and dried

2 tbsp (24 g) sour cream

 30 Minutes or Less

 6+ Grams Net Carbs

 Prep time: 12 minutes

 Cook time: 10 minutes

Serves: 4

Weight: 6.9 oz (194 g) per serving

Net Carbs
6 g

Protein
19 g

Fat
26 g

 343 Calories

 13 g total carbs

 7 g fiber

Creamy Shrimp and Wild Rice Risotto

3 g net carbs

This comforting risotto makes a great light lunch or quick supper. Savory seasoned shrimp are browned in butter before being simmered in a cream sauce. Seasoned cauliflower "rice" is paired with finely minced mushrooms to create a dish with the look and texture of wild rice. A slice of Garlic-Herb Bread (page 161) and Parmesan-Roasted Tomatoes (page 182) are a perfect match.

In a small mixing bowl, toss the jumbo shrimp with the salt, pepper, garlic powder and Italian seasoning.

Melt the butter in a small pan over medium heat. Place the shrimp in the pan and cook on both sides for 2 to 3 minutes. The shrimp should turn pink and start to brown very slightly.

Turn the heat down to low and stir in the heavy cream. Let the shrimp simmer in the cream until the liquid bubbles and thickens, about 1 minute. Take the pan off the heat and set the creamy shrimp aside.

Place the cauliflower rice in a large pan over medium heat with the salt, pepper, rosemary, thyme and onion powder. Cook until the cauliflower releases its liquid and the liquid evaporates. Let the cauliflower turn slightly golden.

Turn the heat to low, and add the butter to the pan, followed by the minced mushrooms. Stir until everything is coated in the butter and heated through.

Finally, stir the grated Parmesan and cooked shrimp into the cream sauce. Fold the ingredients over in the pan until the shrimp has heated through. Garnish with the chopped parsley.

Shrimp

16 pieces peeled and deveined jumbo shrimp

¼ tsp salt

¼ tsp pepper

¼ tsp garlic powder

½ tsp Italian seasoning

1 tbsp (14 g) butter

2 tbsp (30 ml) heavy cream

Wild Rice

2 cups (226 g) fresh or frozen cauliflower rice

½ tsp salt

¼ tsp pepper

½ tsp dried rosemary

¼ tsp dried thyme

½ tsp onion powder

3 tbsp (42 g) butter

4 large cremini mushrooms, minced

3 tbsp (22 g) grated Parmesan

2 tbsp (8 g) chopped parsley

30 Minutes or Less

Prep time: 8 minutes

Cook time: 16 minutes

Serves: 4

Weight: 4.2 oz (121 g) per serving

Net Carbs
3 g

Protein
11 g

Fat
16 g

210 Calories

6 g total carbs

2 g fiber

Salmon Burgers with Wasabi Mayo

3 g net carbs

A proper salmon burger really can't be beat! These perfect patties are bound with keto-friendly ingredients before being cooked to a golden brown. A pungent wasabi mayo is smeared across the burgers before they're topped with the crowd-favorite avocado. Forget the buns; an iceberg lettuce wrap is just as nice. Serve with Radish, Cabbage and Sesame Slaw (page 177).

Pat the salmon dry with a paper towel. Remove the skin if necessary. Add the salmon to a food processor along with the salt, pepper, onion powder, garlic powder, almond flour, Parmesan cheese, gochujang and mayonnaise. Pulse until the mixture has a smooth, burger-like consistency.

Take the salmon burger meat out of the food processor and divide it into four equal portions. Form each portion into a ball.

Heat the avocado oil in a skillet over medium-high heat. When the oil is hot, place the salmon burgers into the skillet, and press them down into a ½-inch (13-mm)-thick burger with the back of a spatula. Place a lid or splatter screen over the skillet and cook the burgers for 4 to 5 minutes per side, or until cooked through. Set the burgers aside to rest.

To make the wasabi mayonnaise, in a small dish, combine the mayonnaise and the wasabi powder. Set aside.

Cut the hard ends away from each outer leaf from a head or two of iceberg lettuce. Make four stacks of two leaves each, and place a salmon burger in the center of each lettuce stack. Smear a portion of wasabi mayo across each burger.

Arrange the avocado slices on each burger. To wrap your burger, fold the top and bottom edges of the lettuce over each burger, followed by the left and right sides. Flip the wraps over so the edges of the lettuce are tucked under the burgers. Then, simply pick up and take a bite to enjoy!

Burgers

18 oz (510 g) salmon

½ tsp salt

½ tsp pepper

¼ tsp onion powder

¼ tsp garlic powder

2 tbsp (15 g) almond flour

½ cup (56 g) shredded Parmesan cheese

1 tsp gochujang (Korean chili paste, see note on page 8)

4 tsp (17 g) mayonnaise

4 tbsp (60 ml) avocado oil

Wasabi Mayo

4 tsp (17 g) mayonnaise

1 tsp wasabi powder

Toppings

8 large outer leaves iceberg lettuce

1 medium avocado, thinly sliced

30 Minutes
or Less

Prep time:
15 minutes

Cook time:
12 minutes

Serves: 4

Weight: 6.1 oz (174 g) per serving

Net Carbs
3 g

Protein
35 g

Fat
39 g

500
Calories

6 g total carbs

2 g fiber

Citrus Salmon

2 g net carbs

If you're craving fruity flavors, just a pinch of orange zest elevates basic salmon to a highly flavorful and enticing meal component. Butter and a smidge of honey, which acts to emulsify the ingredients and help them stick to the salmon, gives the fish a crispy coating. If you are following a strict keto diet, feel free to leave out the honey, in which case we recommend dividing the butter in half and using half to brush on the salmon and half to drizzle on the salmon after it has been cooked. Leaving out the honey reduces the net carbs per serving by 1 gram and the calories per serving by 5 calories. This salmon pairs well with Kimchi Fried Cauli-Rice (page 166) or Toasted Sesame Shirataki Noodles (page 162).

Preheat the oven to 375°F (190°C). Drizzle the olive oil in four portions on a seasoned sheet tray and lay a salmon fillet over each portion. Sprinkle the salt, pepper and garlic powder over the salmon.

Melt the butter in a small dish in the microwave for 20 to 30 seconds or in a small pan on the stovetop over low heat. Stir the honey and orange zest into the melted butter. Use a marinade brush to spread the orange-honey butter over the top and sides of the salmon fillets.

Bake the salmon for 20 to 25 minutes or just until the salmon flakes. Spoon any extra butter over the salmon before serving.

2 tsp (10 ml) olive oil

16 oz (454 g) salmon, divided into 4 portions

½ tsp salt

½ tsp pepper

½ tsp garlic powder

2 tbsp (28 g) butter

1 tsp honey

1 tsp orange zest

Keto Coach Says:

Wild fatty fish like salmon and grass-fed meats are high in omega-3 fatty acids, which may help increase our good cholesterol and reduce triglycerides. Grass-fed organic meats are an excellent choice for many diets because not only do they contain higher amounts of omega-3s, they also don't have the potential harmful effects of antibiotics or pesticides, passed down from the animal's food.

30 Minutes or Less

Prep time: 5 minutes

Cook time: 25 minutes

Serves: 4

Weight: 3 oz (85 g) per serving

Net Carbs
 2 g

Protein
25 g

Fat
16 g

252 Calories

2 g total carbs

<1 g fiber

Thai Omelette

4 g net carbs

30 Minutes or Less   Dairy Free   Paleo

Quick and easy, this Thai Omelette is equally at home as a light dinner or a savory breakfast. For variety, you can substitute ground pork for the shrimp or add additional minced vegetables. If you do not have a wok, you can use a small skillet. If you're making more than two servings, we recommend preparing each omelette separately. A side salad dressed with Creamy Citrus-Avocado Dressing (page 147) would be a great addition.

 Prep time:
10 minutes

 Cook time:
10 minutes

 Serves: 2

Crack the eggs into a small bowl and whisk with the fish sauce. Mix the shrimp with the salt and pepper. Have all of the ingredients close to the stove.

Heat a wok over high heat for 1 to 2 minutes. When hot, add the avocado oil and swirl it around the pan. The oil should shimmer. Add the ginger and green onions , reserving a few green onion slices for garnish, and stir-fry for 30 seconds. Add the shrimp and continue stir-frying until the shrimp starts to turn bright pink but is not fully cooked through. Pour the eggs into the wok, covering the shrimp, ginger and green onion. Do not stir. There should be enough oil in the pan that it bubbles around the edges of the egg and the egg starts to crisp and turn golden brown. After 1 to 2 minutes, use a slotted spatula to flip the omelette over and cook the other side for an additional minute.

Remove the omelette to a plate using the slotted spatula and drizzle with hot sauce to serve.

4 eggs

1 tsp fish sauce

4 oz (113 g) diced raw shrimp

¼ tsp salt

⅛ tsp pepper

2 tbsp (30 ml) avocado oil

1 tsp minced fresh ginger

2 green onions, thinly sliced

1 tsp Sriracha or preferred hot sauce, to serve

Weight: 9 oz (255 g) per serving

Net Carbs
 4 g

Protein
 21 g

Fat
25 g

328 Calories

 4 g total carbs

1 g fiber

Prosciutto, Parmesan and Arugula Tagliatelle

3 g net carbs

This quick and easy dish is rich with tangy Parmesan cheese, salty prosciutto and tender zucchini pasta ribbons that have the texture of handmade fresh pasta. This is a belly-pleasing option for weeknight dinners served with a simple salad or Garlic-Herb Bread (page 161).

Slice the ends from the zucchini. Peel the skin and discard it. Peel the zucchini flesh into long, wide ribbons and set aside.

Heat the olive oil in a skillet over a low-medium heat. Crush the garlic and add it to the skillet, cooking gently until tender. Roughly tear the prosciutto and add it to the pan.

Increase the heat to medium and cook for 1 to 2 minutes, until the edges of the prosciutto are browned. Add the zucchini ribbons to the skillet along with 2 tablespoons (15 g) of the Parmesan and season with salt and pepper. Stir well to combine and cook for 2 to 3 minutes, until the zucchini ribbons are tender and the cheese has melted.

Remove from the heat and stir in the arugula. Sprinkle with the remaining 2 tablespoons (15 g) of Parmesan to serve.

2 large zucchini

2 tbsp (30 ml) olive oil

2 cloves garlic

8 slices (4 oz [113 g]) thinly sliced prosciutto

4 tbsp (30 g) shaved Parmesan, divided

⅛ tsp salt

⅛ tsp black pepper

1 cup (20 g) arugula

Make It Fast:

Use premade or purchased zucchini spirals. Trader Joe's is a good place to find them if they are not available in your local supermarket.

30 Minutes or Less

Prep time: 10 minutes

Cook time: 8 minutes

Serves: 4

Weight: 4.6 oz (130 g) per serving

Net Carbs
3 g

Protein
11 g

Fat
12 g

162 Calories

5 g total carbs

2 g fiber

Walnut and Blue Cheese Spaghetti

5 g net carbs

This quick and easy vegetarian spaghetti is loaded with flavor from creamy blue cheese, aromatic rosemary, protein-rich kale and crunchy toasted walnuts on top. If you'd like to try a variation, the zucchini noodles could be swapped out for cabbage noodles or any other low-carb "spaghetti." Try with Cream of Cauliflower Soup (page 148) for a light vegetarian meal.

Slice the ends from the zucchini. Peel the skin and discard it. Peel the zucchini flesh into long, thin ribbons and set aside.

Add the walnuts to a dry skillet over low-medium heat and toast gently for 2 to 3 minutes until warm and golden.

Melt the butter in a large saucepan over low-medium heat. Add the onion, rosemary and garlic, sweating gently until all of the ingredients are tender and fragrant.

Add the zucchini noodles and stir to coat in the butter and flavorings.

Add the kale to the pan along with 1 tablespoon (8 g) of the blue cheese. Stir well to combine and cook for a few minutes over medium heat, just long enough to wilt the kale, melt the cheese and heat the zucchini. Stir well at the end to ensure the melted cheese is evenly distributed.

Divide the noodles among serving bowls and crumble the toasted walnuts and remaining 2 tablespoons (17 g) of blue cheese over each bowl.

2 large zucchini

¼ cup (20 g) walnuts

2 tbsp (28 g) unsalted butter

1 small red onion, thinly sliced

2 tsp (2 g) fresh rosemary, finely chopped

2 cloves garlic, crushed

1 cup (65 g) Tuscan kale, roughly torn into bite-size chunks

3 tbsp (25 g) crumbled blue cheese, divided

 30 Minutes or Less

 Vegetarian

 Prep time: 12 minutes

 Cook time: 10 minutes

 Serves: 4

Weight: 4.1 oz (116 g) per serving

Net Carbs
5 g

Protein
6 g

Fat
14 g

172 Calories

 8 g total carbs

 2 g fiber

Charred Steak and Mushroom Lettuce Wraps

3 g net carb

Healthy, crunchy lettuce wraps are filled with charred steak, sliced mushrooms and just the right amount of melty mozzarella cheese. This low-carb lunch has protein to curb your hunger and mayonnaise to add a boost of fat.

Season the skirt steak with ½ teaspoon each of salt, pepper and onion powder.

Heat 2 teaspoons (10 ml) of olive oil in a skillet on high heat. When the oil is hot enough to sizzle, add the skirt steak to the pan. Place a lid over the skillet, and cook the steak for 6 to 7 minutes per side. Your steak should be at least medium-well for this recipe. Remove the cooked steak from the skillet and set aside to rest. When the steak has cooled, chop or shred the meat into small pieces.

While the steak is resting, return the pan used to cook the steak to the stove over medium-low heat. Add 2 teaspoons (10 ml) of olive oil and the mushrooms, ¼ teaspoon of salt, ¼ teaspoon of pepper and the paprika. Cook the mushrooms for 3 to 4 minutes, until tender and browned.

Sprinkle the mozzarella cheese over the hot mushrooms and turn off the heat. Place a lid over the skillet so the cheese melts.

Arrange sets of two lettuce leaves each by overlapping the thick ends. Spread ½ tablespoon (7 g) of mayonnaise across the center of each set. Place a portion of shredded steak in the center of each lettuce set. Follow by arranging portions of cheesy mushrooms over the steak.

Fold the top and bottom of each lettuce set over the steak filling, followed by the left and right sides. Flip the wraps over to tuck the edges of the lettuce under the wraps. You may slice the wraps in half, or enjoy like you would a burrito.

16 oz (454 g) skirt steak

¾ tsp salt, divided

¾ tsp pepper, divided

½ tsp onion powder

4 tsp (20 ml) olive oil, divided

6 oz (170 g) cremini mushrooms, thinly sliced

½ tsp paprika

½ cup (56 g) shredded mozzarella cheese

8 large leaves iceberg lettuce, hard ends cut away

2 tbsp (28 g) mayonnaise

Make It New:

Butter lettuce, crisp romaine or any lettuce that you prefer can substitute for iceberg lettuce. Try adding a little mustard or hot sauce with the mayonnaise for additional flavor.

30 Minutes or Less

Prep time: 8 minutes

Cook time: 20 minutes

Serves: 4

Weight: 5.3 oz (150 g) per serving

Net Carbs
3 g

Protein
27 g

Fat
28 g

379 Calories

4 g total carbs

1 g fiber

Chicken Burrito Bowls with Lime Crema

5 g net carbs

Part of what makes this burrito bowl so satisfying is the multiple components that add layers of flavor. It features a quick citrus crema and lots of toppings to add keto fats and extra flavor to your meal. It makes a delicious weeknight dinner or to-go lunch.

Pat the chicken breasts dry with a paper towel, then slice each horizontally into three or four thin fillets. Season with the salt, pepper, cumin, paprika and onion powder.

Heat the olive oil in a medium-sized pan over medium heat. Place the chicken in the oil and put a lid over the pan. Cook the chicken for 4 to 5 minutes per side, until the chicken is golden brown on all sides. Set the cooked chicken aside to cool.

Return the same pan to the stove over medium heat. Toss in the cauliflower rice with the salt, pepper, oregano and paprika. Heat the rice until the cauliflower releases its liquid, deglazes your pan and turns golden brown in the spices and oil leftover in the pan, about 4 minutes. Turn the heat to low and add the lime juice. Add the butter to the rice and stir until coated. Sprinkle the cheese on top of the rice and heat until the cheese has melted. Set aside the finished rice.

Whisk together the sour cream, lime juice and minced cilantro in a small bowl.

Slice the chicken into bite-sized pieces. Divide the lettuce, grape tomatoes, avocado, chicken, cauliflower rice and crema among the four bowls. Serve with lime wedges.

Chicken

2 large chicken breasts (about 14 oz [397 g])

½ tsp salt

½ tsp pepper

½ tsp cumin

½ tsp paprika

¼ tsp onion powder

6 tsp (30 ml) olive oil

Rice

12 oz (336 g) fresh or frozen cauliflower rice

¼ tsp salt

¼ tsp pepper

1 tsp dried oregano

½ tsp paprika

1 tsp lime juice

1 tbsp (14 g) butter

1 cup (115 g) shredded cheddar cheese

Crema

4 tbsp (48 g) sour cream

2 tsp (10 ml) lime juice

¼ cup (4 g) cilantro, minced

Toppings

2 oz (57 g) shredded lettuce

3 oz (85 g) grape tomatoes, diced

5 oz (142 g) avocado, mashed

Lime wedges, for serving

30 Minutes or Less

Prep time: 15 minutes

Cook time: 15 minutes

Serves: 4

Weight: 7.3 oz (206 g) per serving

Net Carbs
5 g

Protein
30 g

Fat
31 g

426 Calories

11 g total carbs

5 g fiber

Thai Spicy Peanut Chicken with Asian Slaw

5 g net carbs

This Thai-inspired chicken dish is a little spicy, a little nutty from some peanut butter and tossed with fresh herbs. Thai basil—if you can find it—will add a hint of sweet licorice flavor, but any type of basil will work. A cool and creamy Asian slaw is paired on the side to counteract any heat from the chili sauce. You can easily double this recipe for multiple days of meals.

In a bowl, combine the coleslaw mix, salt, vinegar, mayonnaise, sesame seeds and lime juice. Set the slaw mixture aside, to give the salt time to draw the moisture out of the coleslaw mix.

Trim and chop the chicken into 1-inch (3-cm) cubes.

Heat the olive oil in a 12-inch (30-cm) skillet on medium-high heat. Add the chicken and black pepper, and cook until the chicken just cooks through, about 7 minutes.

Use a wooden spoon to move the chicken to the outer edges of the pan and turn the heat to very low. Place the peanut butter, sambal oelek and soy sauce in the exposed center of the pan. Let the heat melt the peanut butter slightly, then stir and combine the chicken and the sauce ingredients into a consistent and creamy mixture.

Turn off the heat and stir in the cilantro and basil.

Serve the hot chicken with the coleslaw and a lime wedge. You can add extra cilantro as a garnish at your discretion. Enjoy!

Slaw

2 cups (124 g) packaged coleslaw mix

½ tsp salt

2 tsp (10 ml) rice vinegar

2 tbsp (28 g) mayonnaise

½ tsp sesame seeds

1½ tsp (8 ml) lime juice

Chicken

1¼ lbs (566 g) boneless, skinless chicken breast

1 tbsp (15 ml) olive oil

½ tsp black pepper

2 tbsp (32 g) peanut butter

2 tbsp (30 g) sambal oelek chili sauce

2 tbsp (30 ml) soy sauce

1 tbsp (1 g) cilantro, plus more for garnish (optional)

8 leaves basil, torn

4 lime wedges

30 Minutes or Less   Dairy Free

 Prep time:
10 minutes

 Cook time:
15 minutes

 Serves: 4

Weight: 5.4 oz (152 g) per serving

Net Carbs
5 g

Protein
34 g

Fat
25 g

388 Calories

 10 g total carbs

 4 g fiber

splendid suppers

Sometimes you need a recipe that inspires, a dish that gives a feeling of "Wow!" when you bring it to the table. All of these recipes, while still easy to make, are perfect for weekend evenings or any night when you have a little more time and want something stunning for the table.

A few techniques you will learn when you cook these recipes— like spatchcocking a game hen in the Orange-Glazed Cornish Hens with Broccoli Rabe (page 80) or breading chicken cutlets with pork rinds in the Chicken-Fried Steak Cutlets (page 89)— can, once mastered, be used to make your own recipes. Try spatchcocking a chicken or breading pork cutlets in pork rinds for a keto tonkatsu (Japanese pork cutlet).

Other recipes are just solid family favorites: Monterey Chicken (page 86), crispy wings with a smoky mayo (Crispy Cajun Wings with Paprika Mayo, page 76) or satisfying lamb kebabs (Lamb Kebab Meatball Plate, page 90).

One question that comes up frequently on the Carb Manager message boards is, "Can I eat out at a restaurant and stay keto?" While the recipes in this chapter offer an alternative to eating out for a festive meal, if you find yourself at a restaurant that does not offer a low-carb meal, don't be afraid.

Restaurants are often willing to substitute vegetables or a salad for a starchy side. Look for a protein that is cooked without breading, preferably a fattier cut or with the skin on. Short ribs, chicken thighs, salmon and burgers served over salads are all possible options. Don't be afraid to add butter to your dish or ask for olive oil to drizzle over the vegetables. Finally, restaurants often will add protein to a salad for an extra charge— hold the croutons and ask for oil and vinegar if you're not sure about the salad dressing.

You can find most chain restaurant menu items as well as common dishes on the Carb Manager app for tracking your net carbs and other macros.

Crispy Cajun Wings with Paprika Mayo

2 g net carbs

These Cajun-inspired wings are coated in aromatic dried herbs and spices then oven baked until the skin is crisp and golden. The smoky paprika dip provides a substantial amount of fat and could double as a dip for vegetables or a drizzle for a salad. If you would like to make this recipe using frozen wings, increase the cooking time to 50 minutes, turning the wings once at 30 minutes. These are a great sharing meal for friends and family—perfect for the holidays or lazy weekends. Serve the wings with the dip and a simple green vegetable or salad. Sheet Pan Zucchini (page 174) can be baked at the same time as the chicken wings (reduce baking time of zucchini to 25 minutes to account for the higher temperature) and makes an easy side.

Preheat the oven to 400°F (200°C). Line a sheet pan with tin foil.

Add the chicken wings to a large mixing bowl with the salt, pepper, paprika, garlic powder, onion powder, oregano, thyme, cumin, cayenne, lime juice, lime zest and olive oil. Use your hands to thoroughly rub the seasonings and oil all over the chicken. Arrange the wings in an even layer across the foil-lined sheet pan.

Transfer to the oven to bake for 30 minutes, or until the chicken is cooked through and the skin is crisp and golden.

To prepare the dip, add the mayonnaise, sour cream, paprika, cumin, lime juice, salt and pepper to a small bowl and whisk together until smooth and combined.

Crispy Wings

2 lbs (907 g) chicken wings

½ tsp salt

⅛ tsp black pepper

2 tsp (5 g) smoked paprika

1 tsp garlic powder

1 tsp onion powder

2 tsp (2 g) dried oregano

1 tsp dried thyme

1 tsp ground cumin

½ tsp cayenne pepper (or to taste)

1 tsp lime juice

1 tsp lime zest

1 tbsp (15 ml) olive oil

Paprika Dip

1 tbsp (14 g) mayonnaise

1 tbsp (12 g) sour cream

1 tsp smoked paprika

½ tsp ground cumin

1 tsp lime juice

¼ tsp sea salt

⅛ tsp black pepper

Prep time:
10 minutes

Cook time:
30 minutes

Serves: 4

Weight: 4 oz (113 g) per serving

Net Carbs
 2 g

Protein
54 g

Fat
45 g

647 Calories

3 g total carbs

1 g fiber

Sheet Pan Chicken Thighs with Sweet Peppers and Olives

6 g net carbs

These crispy chicken thighs are baked with sweet and slightly spicy peppadew peppers and juicy olives until perfectly golden then served on a bed of lemony cauliflower rice. A simple green salad dressed with Mixed Berry Poppyseed Vinaigrette (page 143) would round out the meal.

Preheat the oven to 375°F (190°C).

In a small mixing bowl, combine the garlic, olive oil, lemon zest and dried oregano.

Arrange the chicken thighs across a sheet pan and sprinkle with the salt and pepper, then drizzle with the marinade. Use your hands to rub the marinade into the chicken. Transfer the sheet pan to the oven to bake for 20 minutes.

Remove the sheet pan from the oven and add the green olives, black olives and peppadew peppers to the tray with the partly cooked chicken, basting the thighs with any pan juices. Return the pan to the oven for an additional 15 minutes, or until the chicken is cooked through and the skin is crisp and golden.

While the chicken finishes cooking, add the cauliflower rice to a saucepan along with the water and lemon juice. Bring to a simmer and cook until all the liquid has evaporated and the cauliflower is hot through.

Serve the cauliflower rice alongside the baked chicken, olives and peppers, spooning the pan juices over the top to serve.

1 clove garlic, crushed

1 tbsp (15 ml) olive oil

1 tsp lemon zest

2 tsp (2 g) dried oregano

4 large chicken thighs, bone in and skin on

½ tsp sea salt

⅛ tsp black pepper

½ cup (80 g) large green olives

⅓ cup (55 g) black olives

½ cup (45 g) peppadew peppers

4 cups (455 g) fresh or frozen cauliflower rice

¼ cup (60 ml) water

1 tsp lemon juice

Make It New:

Try adding chopped kale or canned artichoke hearts to the sheet pan when you add olives or peppers. Experiment with spices and herbs—fresh or dried thyme is a great addition, as is a sprinkle of chili flakes.

6+ Grams Net Carbs   Dairy Free   Paleo

Prep time: 7 minutes

Cook time: 35 minutes

Serves: 4

Weight: 8 oz (227 g) per serving

Net Carbs
6 g

Protein
33 g

Fat
22 g

370 Calories

11 g total carbs

5 g fiber

Orange-Glazed Cornish Hens with Broccoli Rabe

3 g net carbs

A Cornish hen is the perfect size to share between two people. If you've never spatchcocked a bird before, do not be intimidated; a little Cornish game hen is the perfect bird to use to learn the technique. Because of its small size, it is easy to cut through the backbone and, once you feel confident with this recipe, you can use the same technique on a chicken or even a turkey for a quick-cooking meal with perfect skin. This hen has a crispy skin that is aromatic with dried herbs, garlic and just the right amount of orange zest. Served over a ginger-flavored bed of broccoli rabe, this is a complete meal.

Preheat the oven to 400°F (200°C) and line a sheet tray with parchment paper.

To spatchcock the Cornish hen, cut out the backbone with kitchen shears (be sure to use poultry shears if you try this on a turkey!) and push down on the breast bone so the bird is splayed out with all the skin on top. Repeat with the second hen. Rub the olive oil into the meat, then rub on the salt, pepper, onion powder, oregano and rosemary. Be sure to cover all of the meat, including under the wings.

Set the spatchcocked Cornish hens on the parchment-lined sheet tray. Bake the birds for 30 minutes.

While the birds are baking, prepare the orange glaze. Whisk together the melted butter, orange juice and zest and garlic; set aside.

Boil water in a large pot on the stovetop. While it's coming to a boil, prepare an ice water bath by filling a large bowl with cold water and ice. Once boiling, add the salt and the broccoli rabe and cook for 3 minutes, then rapidly chill in cold water and drain.

(continued)

Cornish Hens

2 lbs (907 g) Cornish hen (2 hens)

3 tsp (15 ml) olive oil

½ tsp salt

¼ tsp pepper

¼ tsp onion powder

½ tsp dried oregano

½ tsp dried rosemary

Orange Glaze

4 tbsp (56 g) butter, melted

2 tbsp (30 ml) orange juice

1½ tbsp (8 g) fresh orange zest

3 tsp (9 g) minced garlic

Broccoli Rabe

1 tsp salt

12 oz (336 g) broccoli rabe

3 tbsp (45 ml) olive oil

½ tsp pepper

2 tsp (6 g) sesame seeds

1 oz (28 g) grated ginger root

 Prep time: 25 minutes

 Cook time: 65 minutes

 Serves: 4

Weight: 8.9 oz (252 g) per serving

Net Carbs
 3 g

Protein
42 g

Fat
58 g

 718 Calories

 7 g total carbs

 3 g fiber

Orange-Glazed Cornish Hens
with Broccoli Rabe (continued)

After the first 30 minutes of baking, brush one-third of the glaze over the birds. Bake the birds for another 15 minutes. After 15 minutes, brush the birds with another one-third of the glaze. Bake for 10 more minutes. Brush with the remaining glaze and bake for 10 more minutes, or until the internal temperature reaches 160°F (70°C) using a meat thermometer, resulting in about 65 minutes total baking time. Let the birds rest until serving time.

Transfer the blanched broccoli rabe to a saucepan with the olive oil, pepper, sesame seeds and ginger. Cook the greens over medium heat for about 5 minutes.

For serving, arrange the broccoli rabe on a large plate. Place the Cornish hens directly on top of the broccoli rabe.

Keto Coach Says:

Plants make useful compounds called phytochemicals, which give fruits and vegetables their color. The color of the fruit or veggie indicates a high concentration of a particular phytochemical. In our bodies, phytochemicals may contribute to health by boosting the immune system, reducing inflammation, preventing DNA damage, regulating hormone and gene expression, reducing oxidative stress and more!

Breaded Meatballs with Pesto Noodles

9 g net carbs

These pork meatballs are loaded with Italian seasoning, coated in a ground almond crumb and baked until crisp and golden. They are served with tender cabbage noodles in a sun-dried tomato pesto sauce. This is a crowd-pleasing weekend option for families! Pine Nut Biscotti (page 231) is a perfect dessert.

Add the ground pork to a mixing bowl with the salt and pepper, ½ tablespoon (1.5 g) of the Italian seasoning and the garlic powder. Use your hands to mix together thoroughly.

Roll the mixture into 20 meatballs.

Preheat the oven to 400°F (200°C). Lightly grease a shallow sheet pan with cooking spray.

Whisk the egg in a small bowl. Add the almond flour to a separate bowl with a pinch of salt and pepper and the remaining ½ tablespoon (1.5 g) of the Italian seasoning. Stir to combine.

Roll each meatball in the beaten egg so that it is well coated and then dredge in the seasoned almond flour so the meatballs are covered all over.

Arrange the breaded meatballs on the greased sheet pan. Bake for 18 minutes or until cooked through and golden.

While the meatballs are baking, add the sun-dried tomatoes, pine nuts, Parmesan cheese, garlic, lemon zest, basil and pepper to a food processor and blend to combine.

Add the olive oil, a little at a time, with the motor of the food processor still running, blending until you have a semi-smooth consistency.

(continued)

Meatballs

17.5 oz (500 g) ground pork

¼ tsp sea salt, plus more to taste

⅛ tsp black pepper, plus more to taste

1 tbsp (3 g) Italian seasoning, divided

½ tsp garlic powder

1 medium egg

1 cup (96 g) almond flour

Pesto Noodles

6 sun-dried tomatoes

1 tbsp (8 g) pine nuts

1 tbsp (7 g) grated Parmesan cheese

1 clove garlic

1 tsp lemon zest

½ cup (12 g) fresh basil

⅛ tsp black pepper

⅓ cup (80 ml) olive oil

1 lb (454 g) head cabbage

½ cup (120 ml) vegetable stock

6+ Grams
Net Carbs

Prep time:
25 minutes

Cook time:
25 minutes

Serves: 4

Weight: 10.3 oz (292 g) per serving

Net Carbs
9 g

Protein
44 g

Fat
62 g

772
Calories

15 g total carbs

6 g fiber

Breaded Meatballs with
Pesto Noodles (continued)

Remove the tough core from the cabbage and discard any wilted outer leaves. Slice the cabbage into ½-inch (13-mm)-thick ribbons and add to a large pan with the stock. Bring to a gentle boil over medium-high heat and simmer for 5 to 6 minutes, until the cabbage is fork tender and the liquid has almost all evaporated.

Add the pesto, stir to combine and warm through.

Arrange the meatballs atop the noodles to serve.

Keto Coach Says:

Tracking macros by hand can be a frustrating and confusing process. The nutrition information on food packaging rounds to the nearest whole number for the typical serving size. For some items, like heavy cream, that means that one serving (1 tbsp or 15 ml) may have 0 g carbs listed on the packaging, but the actual number is 0.4 g. This can add up quickly if you add a few tablespoons of cream to the recipe!

If you need to be more accurate, we recommend using Carb Manager to track your macros. It's always important to look at the whole picture. For instance, Breaded Meatballs with Pesto Noodles may have 9 g of carbs, but it's a well-balanced keto meal when the protein, fat and calories are considered.

Monterey Chicken

3 g net carbs

There are many variations of Monterey Chicken, but they all include some tasty staples: a smear of barbecue sauce, melted cheese and a bit of bacon! This family-friendly version uses boneless, skinless thighs instead of the usual breasts for more flavor and fat. The fresh and slightly spicy avocado topping adds contrast. Baked Cauliflower "Mac and Cheese" (page 169) goes well with this dish.

Preheat the oven to 375°F (190°C). Drizzle the olive oil in a 9 x 13–inch (23 x 33–cm) glass baking dish. Pat the chicken thighs dry and place them in the olive oil. Flip so both sides are covered with oil. Spread 1 teaspoon of BBQ sauce across the top of each thigh.

Sprinkle the salt, pepper, onion powder, garlic powder, paprika and cumin across the chicken thighs. Bake the thighs, uncovered, for 20 minutes.

After 20 minutes, remove the dish from the oven. Arrange about a tablespoon (6 g) of cheddar cheese over each chicken thigh and sprinkle the bacon bits over the cheese. Return the dish to the oven to bake for a final 10 minutes.

While the chicken is baking, make the avocado topping. Stir together the grape tomatoes, jalapeño, cilantro and avocado in a small bowl.

Arrange the Monterey Chicken on a serving dish. Top each chicken thigh with an equal amount of the avocado topping.

2 tbsp (30 ml) olive oil

1 lb (454 g) boneless, skinless chicken thighs

4 tsp (20 ml) BBQ sauce

½ tsp salt

¼ tsp pepper

¼ tsp onion powder

¼ tsp garlic powder

¼ tsp paprika

¼ tsp cumin

¼ cup (25 g) shredded cheddar cheese

2 tbsp (14 g) bacon bits

Avocado Topping

4 grape tomatoes, diced

½ small jalapeño, diced

2 tsp (1 g) chopped cilantro

4 oz (113 g) avocado

 Prep time:
10 minutes

 Cook time:
30 minutes

 Serves: 4

Weight: 4.3 oz (123 g) per serving

Net Carbs
 3 g

Protein
 26 g

Fat
 19 g

 296 Calories

 6 g total carbs

2 g fiber

Chicken-Fried Steak Cutlets

2 g net carbs

Pork rinds are a keto hack to add fat and crunch without needing to deep-fry. They also happen to make the perfect "breading" for recipes such as this one. Enjoy as is for a tasty dinner with a side dish, or enjoy as a sandwich with your favorite keto bun and spicy peppers. We recommend Buttermilk Biscuits (page 158) and a scoop of Superfood Keto Salad (page 132) on the side.

Preheat the oven to 375°F (190°C). Arrange the thin slices of steak on a flat surface. Sprinkle the salt and pepper over the steak.

To make the breading, combine the pork rinds, almond flour, paprika, garlic powder and onion powder in a food processor. Pulse until you have a fine crumb.

Line a sheet tray with parchment paper. Whisk the egg in a dish. Transfer the breading from the food processor to a plate.

Dip the seasoned steak cutlets into the egg, allow the egg to drip off, then press into the breading. Arrange each breaded steak cutlet on the parchment-lined sheet tray.

Bake the steak for 60 minutes, flipping the slices over after 40 minutes. The steak will be browned and crispy.

1 lb (454 g) top round steak, sliced approximately ¼ inch (6 mm) thin (see Note)

¼ tsp salt

½ tsp pepper

1½ cups (50 g) pork rinds

¼ cup (28 g) almond flour

1 tsp paprika

1 tsp garlic powder

½ tsp onion powder

1 medium egg

Note:

Specify "cutlets" or "sandwich steak" to your butcher to ensure the steak is sliced horizontally in large, thin steaks. Alternately, you can place your steak in the freezer for 45 minutes or until partially frozen and carefully slice to create large, thin cutlets. The number of steaks will vary depending on the size of the initial piece, but you should have around 4 to 6 slices.

 Dairy Free
 Paleo

Prep time:
15 minutes

Cook time:
60 minutes

Serves: 4

Weight: 3.2 oz (91 g) per serving

Net Carbs
2 g

Protein
34 g

Fat
19 g

321 Calories

 3 g total carbs

 1 g fiber

Lamb Kebab Meatball Plate

3 g net carbs

Your kitchen is going to smell heavenly from this fragrant blend of spices baking in your oven. Ground lamb is seasoned with classic Mediterranean spices before being rolled into meatballs and baked on a rack. The fresh flavors of the cucumber tomato salad offer a perfect balance. Strawberry, Lime and Basil Granita (page 236) would work well for dessert.

If you plan to use wooden skewers, soak them in water for at least 20 minutes before you begin the recipe.

Preheat the oven to 375°F (190°C). In a mixing bowl, combine the ground lamb, salt, pepper, onion powder, garlic powder, cumin, oregano, parsley and dill. Use your hands to form the mixture into eight meatballs with a slightly oblong, oval shape.

Arrange two meatballs each onto four skewers. Set the skewers on a metal cooling rack, and set the rack over a sheet tray to catch any drippings.

Cook the meatballs in the oven for 35 minutes, or until a meat thermometer inserted into the center of the meatball reads 175°F (80°C). Flip the meatballs over on the rack about halfway through the baking time.

While the meatballs are cooking, make the salad. In a bowl, mix together the cucumber, grape tomatoes, olive oil, lemon juice, salt and fresh dill. Make sure to cover the cucumbers and tomatoes well in the seasonings. Set the bowl aside to marinate until serving time. (For a stronger flavor, you can make this dish a day ahead and allow it to marinate overnight.)

Serve one skewer of lamb meatballs with a quarter of the cucumber side dish.

4 wooden or metal skewers

Meatballs

1 lb (454 g) ground lamb

¼ tsp salt

¼ tsp pepper

¼ tsp onion powder

¼ tsp garlic powder

⅛ tsp ground cumin

½ tsp dried oregano

½ tsp dried parsley

1 tbsp (3 g) dill, freshly chopped

Salad

10 oz (280 g) cucumber, quartered

4 oz (113 g) grape tomatoes, halved

1½ tbsp (22 ml) olive oil

2 tsp (10 ml) lemon juice

¼ tsp salt

2 tsp (2 g) dill, freshly chopped

Dairy Free

Paleo

Prep time:
20 minutes

Cook time:
35 minutes

Serves: 4

Weight: 6.2 oz (177 g) per serving

Net Carbs
3 g

Protein
26 g

Fat
28 g

376
Calories

4 g total carbs

1 g fiber

Spicy Korean Short Ribs with Crispy Cabbage

6 g net carbs

Spicy foods are known to be helpful to aid in digestion and metabolism. These spicy beef short ribs don't skimp on the heat! Seaweed Salad (page 178), Toasted Sesame Shirataki Noodles (page 162) and store-bought kimchi would make good sides.

The day before you want to cook your short ribs, prepare the marinade. In a small bowl, stir together the olive oil, gochujang, salt, pepper and red pepper flakes.

Arrange the boneless short ribs in either a glass dish or a sealable bag. Rub the marinade into the short ribs. You can do this with your hands or use a plastic bag to rub the marinade into the ribs (wash your hands very well afterward as the red pepper flakes and gochujang may irritate your skin). Set the short ribs in the refrigerator to marinate overnight, or at least 12 hours.

When you are ready to cook the short ribs, preheat the oven to 400°F (200°C).

Prepare four cabbage "steaks" by removing the core from a head of cabbage. Cut the head in half and slice 1-inch (3-cm)-thick steaks from the center. Arrange them on a seasoned sheet tray, coated with pan spray if necessary.

Sprinkle the cabbage with the salt, paprika, garlic powder and green onion. Drizzle approximately ¼ teaspoon of rice vinegar and 1 teaspoon of olive oil across each cabbage steak.

Place a single marinated short rib on top of each cabbage steak. Drizzle any remaining marinade you can scrape up over the short ribs.

Bake the cabbage and short ribs for 50 minutes.

To serve, slice each short rib into thin, rectangular slices. Transfer the crispy cabbage and short ribs to each plate.

Short Ribs

1½ tbsp (22 ml) olive oil

1 tbsp (21 g) gochujang (see Note)

¼ tsp salt

¼ tsp pepper

½ tsp red pepper flakes

1½ lbs (680 g) boneless beef short ribs, cut into 4 thin steaks

Crispy Cabbage

14 oz (397 g) head green cabbage

¼ tsp salt

½ tsp paprika

¼ tsp garlic powder

1 medium green onion, chopped, plus more to garnish

1 tsp rice vinegar

4 tsp (20 ml) olive oil

Note:

Most gochujang available in stores is made with barley-malt syrup, sugar or corn syrup. The amount of gochujang in this recipe accounts for 1 gram of carbohydrates per serving. If you leave it out of the marinade, you may want to double the amount of chili flakes.

6+ Grams Net Carbs

Dairy Free

Prep time:
10 minutes + 12 hours marinade time

Cook time:
50 minutes

Serves: 4

Weight: 5.7 oz (161 g) per serving

Net Carbs
 6 g

Protein
31 g

Fat
41 g

520 Calories

9 g total carbs

2 g fiber

Philly Cheesesteak Skillet

2 g net carbs

This has been a #1 hit on Carb Manager. Nothing shouts "comfort food" like a fat, meaty, melty Philly cheesesteak. We may have to skip the bread, but we don't have to skip on the juicy steak and gooey cheese! This one-skillet meal makes for an easy dinner or lunch, and it will warm your belly right up. If you don't own a cast-iron or oven-safe skillet, you can prepare the veggies and steak in a stovetop pan and then transfer the ingredients to a baking dish.

Preheat the oven to 350°F (175°C).

On a clean surface, slice the steak across the grain into 4-inch (10-cm) strips that are about ⅛ inch (3 mm) thick. Heat the olive oil in a large skillet on medium-high heat, and add the steak. Sprinkle the salt, pepper, onion powder and garlic powder over the steak.

Allow the meat to sear in the pan without moving it for a few minutes. Turn the heat to high and cook, stirring occasionally, until the steak starts to crisp. This will take about 12 minutes.

Transfer the cooked steak to a dish. Leave all juices in the skillet. Turn the heat down to medium–low. Add the mushrooms and green bell pepper to the skillet. Cook the vegetables for about 3 minutes, stirring occasionally, until they are just cooked through and browning slightly on the edges. Remove the skillet from the heat.

Return the cooked steak to the skillet, and mix the meat and veggies together. If you do not have an oven-safe skillet, combine the cooked ingredients in an oiled 9 x 12–inch (23 x 30–cm) baking dish.

Arrange the cheese over the top of the cheesesteak ingredients so everything is covered. Bake the ingredients in the oven for about 5 minutes, or until the cheese melts.

To get a slightly browned top, place the skillet under a broiler for an additional 3 to 4 minutes before serving.

Ingredients

1 lb (454 g) flank steak

1½ tbsp (22 ml) olive oil

½ tsp salt

1 tsp ground black pepper

½ tsp onion powder

¼ tsp garlic powder

5 medium white mushrooms, sliced

½ green bell pepper, diced

6 slices provolone cheese

 Prep time: 10 minutes

 Cook time: 25 minutes

 Serves: 4

Weight: 4 oz (113 g) per serving

Net Carbs
 2 g

Protein
 44 g

Fat
○ 24 g

 398 Calories

 3 g total carbs

1 g fiber

Prosciutto Eggplant Parmesan

7 g net carbs

No breading here—these eggplant parms keep a crispy outside thanks to salty slices of prosciutto. A touch of marinara sauce, a hefty sprinkle of Parmesan cheese and a fresh mozzarella salad maintain the classic flavors of this dish. Garlic-Herb Bread (page 161) with a smear of your favorite Compound Butter (page 183) would be a perfect accompaniment.

Preheat the oven to 375°F (190°C). Line a sheet tray with parchment paper.

Slice the eggplant into twelve ¼-inch (6-mm) slices, and arrange the slices on the parchment-lined tray. Sprinkle the eggplant slices with the pepper, Italian seasoning, onion powder and garlic powder. Drizzle the slices with approximately ¼ teaspoon of olive oil each.

Spread approximately ½ teaspoon of marinara sauce over each slice. Wrap a slice of prosciutto around each eggplant slice, tucking the ends of the prosciutto under the slices. Sprinkle 1 teaspoon of Parmesan over each wrapped slice.

Bake the eggplant for 25 minutes, or until the prosciutto is browned at the edges and the eggplant is tender.

While the eggplant is baking, prepare the salad by cutting the tomato into chunks to match the size of the mozzarella pieces and tossing them together with the basil, olive oil and salt in a medium bowl.

Serve the eggplant by placing three slices on each plate with a side of mozzarella salad.

Eggplant

10.6 oz (300 g) eggplant, whole

1 tsp pepper

2 tsp (2 g) Italian seasoning

1 tsp onion powder

1 tsp garlic powder

1 tbsp (15 ml) olive oil

2 tbsp (30 ml) marinara sauce (no sugar)

7 oz (200 g) prosciutto (12 slices)

¼ cup (30 g) grated Parmesan

Salad

1 medium tomato

8 oz (227 g) fresh mozzarella (either ciliegine or cut into 1-inch [3-cm] chunks)

2 tbsp (5 g) chopped basil

2 tbsp (30 ml) extra-virgin olive oil

¼ tsp salt

6+ Grams Net Carbs

Prep time: 15 minutes

Cook time: 25 minutes

Serves: 4 (3 slices per serving)

Weight: 7 oz (200 g) per serving

Net Carbs
 7 g

Protein
 25 g

Fat
27 g

383 Calories

10 g total carbs

3 g fiber

Almond Flounder with Spanish Rice and Salsa

6 g net carbs

Spicy flounder fillets are coated in crunchy almonds and served with a fragrant Spanish cauliflower "rice." To balance the heat, a fresh salsa of cool tomato and avocado is spooned on top. Serve with a side salad or spinach dressed with a Compound Butter (page 183) for a satisfying dinner.

Preheat the oven to 350°F (175°C).

Drizzle the olive oil in four portions on a sheet tray. Lay a flounder fillet over each portion of olive oil. Sprinkle the salt, pepper, cumin, onion powder, red pepper flakes and garlic powder over the fillets.

Press the sliced almonds on top of the fish so they adhere. Bake the tray of flounder for 20 to 25 minutes in the oven, adjusting for the thickness of the fish fillets.

While the fish is baking, make the Spanish rice. Heat the cauliflower rice in a large pan over high heat with the salt, paprika, onion powder and cumin. Stir until the rice turns golden brown and starts to crisp up.

Turn the heat to low. Melt the butter into the rice and stir in the cilantro. Cook until the butter turns the rice slightly darker and the cilantro turns dark green. Set aside.

When the fish is done baking, prepare the salsa. Combine the diced tomatoes, avocado, salt, lime juice and cilantro in a small mixing bowl.

Serve each flounder fillet with cauliflower rice and top with fresh salsa.

Flounder

4 tsp (20 ml) olive oil

11 oz (312 g) flounder fillet

½ tsp salt

½ tsp pepper

1 tsp cumin

½ tsp onion powder

1 tsp red pepper flakes

½ tsp garlic powder

6 tbsp (42 g) sliced almonds

Spanish Rice

20 oz (560 g) fresh or frozen cauliflower rice

1 tsp salt

2 tsp (5 g) paprika

½ tsp onion powder

2 tsp (4 g) cumin

2 tbsp (28 g) butter

4 tbsp (4 g) chopped cilantro

Salsa

8 grape tomatoes, diced

½ medium avocado, diced

¼ tsp salt

2 tsp (10 ml) lime juice

4 tsp (2 g) chopped cilantro

6+ Grams Net Carbs

 Prep time: 9 minutes

 Cook time: 30 minutes

 Serves: 4

Weight: 7 oz (200 g) per serving

Net Carbs
6 g

Protein
15 g

Fat
20 g

 273 Calories

 12 g total carbs

 6 g fiber

Crab Cakes with Spinach and Artichokes

4 g net carbs

These crab cakes are great to make with canned crab, but they are divine with fresh crab when it is in season. This is a simple, special-occasion meal that is quick to put together and easy to make.

Preheat the oven to 375°F (190°C). Line a sheet tray with parchment paper.

In a bowl, mix together the crab, mayonnaise, lemon juice, mustard, green onion, salt, ¼ teaspoon of pepper, paprika, red pepper flakes, garlic powder, parsley and almond flour. Form four crab cakes from the mixture and press them onto the parchment-lined sheet tray.

Bake the crab cakes for 30 minutes, no flipping necessary. They should be browned and crisped around the edges. Set the cakes aside to cool.

While the crab cakes are baking, make the spinach and artichokes. Melt the butter in a pan over low heat. Stir in the spinach, artichoke hearts and ¼ teaspoon of pepper. Place a lid on the pan and let the ingredients cook on low heat for 5 to 7 minutes, until the artichokes are fully heated through and the spinach is wilted.

Stir the heavy cream into the pan. Replace the lid on the pan and bring the heavy cream to a simmer (this will only take about 1 minute). Then, take the pan off the heat and quickly stir the Parmesan cheese into the pan until it melts and thickens the cream.

To serve, make four beds of spinach and artichokes and top them each with a crab cake. You can drizzle any excess butter from your pan over the crab cakes as well.

12 oz (336 g) lump crab, drained if canned

4 tbsp (52 g) mayonnaise

4 tsp (20 ml) lemon juice

4 tsp (20 g) Dijon mustard

1 medium green onion, chopped

½ tsp salt

½ tsp pepper, divided

1 tsp paprika

¼ tsp red pepper flakes

¼ tsp garlic powder

1 tsp dried parsley

⅓ cup (30 g) almond flour

2 tbsp (28 g) butter

2 cups (60 g) spinach, chopped

1 cup (170 g) jarred artichoke hearts, sliced

½ cup (120 ml) heavy cream

6 tbsp (44 g) grated Parmesan

Prep time: 15 minutes

Cook time: 30 minutes

Serves: 4

Weight: 4.4 oz (125 g) per serving

Net Carbs
 4 g

Protein
23 g

Fat
38 g

456 Calories

 8 g total carbs

 3 g fiber

Crispy Tofu Bowl

8 g net carbs

 6+ Grams Net Carbs
 Dairy Free
 Vegetarian

This tofu is coated in a tangy peanut and tamari marinade then baked until golden and served with zesty broccoli rice, tender bok choy and creamy avocado.

Preheat the oven to 400°F (200°C).

Cover the tofu with a clean tea towel or paper towels and weigh it down with a heavy object to press out any excess liquid.

Add the tamari, lime juice, syrup, chili powder, coriander, garlic powder and peanut butter to a small mixing bowl. Whisk together until smooth.

Dice the tofu into chunks roughly ⅔ inch (1.5 cm) wide and place them in a shallow dish or bowl. Add half of the marinade and gently mix. Reserve the rest of the marinade.

Arrange the coated tofu across a parchment-lined pan and bake for 18 to 20 minutes, or until the tofu is crisp and golden.

While the tofu is baking, slice the bok choy in half lengthwise. Rinse well and pat dry. Heat the coconut oil in a skillet over medium heat and add the bok choy, cut side down. Pan-fry for 1 to 2 minutes until golden brown, then add the sliced garlic. Turn the bok choy and brown the other side. Add 2 tablespoons (30 ml) of water to the skillet and cover with a lid. Cook for 2 to 3 minutes, until tender.

Add the broccoli rice to a small saucepan with ¼ cup (60 ml) of water, lime zest, salt and pepper. Simmer for 3 to 4 minutes, until hot through and all the liquid has been absorbed.

To serve, divide the avocados between serving bowls. Add the crispy tofu, bok choy and broccoli rice. Add a teaspoon or so of water to the remaining marinade and whisk. Drizzle over the vegetables. Crumble the coconut flakes over the rice and scatter with the fresh cilantro.

Tofu

18 oz (510 g) extra-firm tofu

2 tbsp (30 ml) tamari sauce

2 tsp (10 ml) lime juice

2 tsp (10 ml) Lakanto maple-flavored syrup

2 tsp (3 g) chili powder

2 tsp (3 g) ground coriander

1 tsp garlic powder

2 tsp (10 g) peanut butter

Bok Choy

2 small stalks bok choy

3 tbsp (40 g) coconut oil

2 cloves garlic, thinly sliced

Broccoli Rice

1⅓ cup (90 g) broccoli rice

2 tsp (4 g) lime zest

½ tsp sea salt

¼ tsp black pepper

Toppings

2 avocados, thinly sliced

4 tsp (4 g) flaked coconut

2 tbsp (2 g) chopped cilantro

Note:

To make broccoli rice, just trim the tips of a head of broccoli with a pair of scissors to give you a rice-like consistency. Or you can use a sharp knife and cutting board to shave the crown.

 Prep time: 20 minutes

 Cook time: 20 minutes

 Serves: 4

Weight: 9.1 oz (258 g) per serving

Net Carbs
8 g

Protein
17 g

Fat
29 g

 368 Calories

 18 g total carbs

 9 g fiber

batch cooking & make aheads

"I love eating keto, but I just don't have time!" "What should I eat for lunch?" "Everyone eats at different times in our family." Have you ever said these things? The solution is to either cook in a large batch or make components of the meal ahead of time for easy assembly. All of the recipes in this chapter can be cooked in a large batch, like the Chili Con Carne (page 122) and Roasted Pork Tenderloin with Caraway Sauerkraut (page 109); made ahead and portioned out, like Spiced Beef Koftas with Tahini Dipping Sauce (page 110) and Coriander-Lime Chicken Kebabs with Radish Salad (page 113); or have a component that can be made in advance then finished at the last minute, like the Vietnamese Lemongrass Pork Noodle Bowl (page 106) and Pepperoni Pizza (page 125).

Flavored Compound Butters (page 183) can also be made ahead and used to elevate a simple meal of a protein and a vegetable into a delightful treat. If you are struggling to add enough fat, these are a quick solution.

Making sure that at least two meals on your weekly meal plan are made ahead can save time in the evening or when packing a lunch for the next day. Any of these recipes work well for lunch, as would leftovers from most of our main dishes or any soup or salad recipe.

freezer meals

The following recipes from throughout the book work well to make ahead and freeze in individual portions for quick meals. Freezing items like pancakes or meatballs on a sheet pan and then transferring to a bag or large container makes portioning a snap.

Breakfast: Blueberry-Lemon Pancakes (page 18), Cinnamon-Flax Almond Muffins (page 28)

Savory Mains: Salmon Burgers with Wasabi Mayo (page 58), Chicken-Fried Steak Cutlets (page 89), Breaded Meatballs with Pesto Noodles (page 83), Spiced Beef Koftas with Tahini Dipping Sauce (page 110), Coriander-Lime Chicken Kebabs with Radish Salad (page 113), Buffalo Chicken Meatballs with Creamy Blue Cheese Dip (page 117), Chili Con Carne (page 122), Cream of Cauliflower Soup (page 148)

Bread & Butter: Pre-baked Pizza Crust (see directions in Pepperoni Pizza recipe on page 125), Buttermilk Biscuits (page 158), Garlic-Herb Bread (page 161), Compound Butters (page 183)

Desserts: Hazelnut Truffle Fat Bombs (page 218), Almond Fat Bomb Fudge (page 221), Coconut, Lime and Raspberry Fat Bombs (page 222), Peanut Butter and Jelly Ice Cream (page 235), Strawberry, Lime and Basil Granita (page 236)

Vietnamese Lemongrass Pork Noodle Bowl

9 g net carbs

This is a low-carb version of the classic lemongrass pork noodle bowl, or *bún*. The noodles are meant to be enjoyed chilled with hot, grilled meat on top. The bowls can be prepped ahead of time, and you can add the grilled meat right before serving. We specify an English cucumber for its thin skin, but any thin-skinned cucumber will work. If you need to use one with thick skin, peel before julienning. Add some chili-garlic sauce if you would like extra heat and garnish with lime wedges.

Slice the pork shoulder into 1-inch (3-cm)-thick steaks. Place the slices in a zip-top plastic bag. Blend the garlic, shallots, erythritol, pepper, dark soy sauce, fish sauce, soy sauce, lemongrass and avocado oil using a stick blender until the lemongrass, garlic and shallots are roughly chopped. Pour the marinade over the pork and allow it to marinate for at least 1 hour, or overnight for the best taste.

Whisk the lime juice, fish sauce, garlic, granulated erythritol and water together in a small bowl.

Remove the tofu noodles from the package and rinse very well. Divide the noodles among four bowls and top them with the julienned carrot and cucumber. You can refrigerate the bowls at this point if you would like to make them ahead of time.

When ready to cook, preheat a grill (or grill pan) over medium-high heat. Grill the pork, cooking on the first side until it releases from the grill evenly, about 4 to 5 minutes. Turn the pork over and cook for another 2 to 3 minutes. Flip again and this time cook until the pork is cooked through and reaches an internal temperature of at least 145°F (65°C). Remove the meat from the grill and allow it to rest for 5 minutes before slicing it thin.

Divide the meat among the bowls and arrange it on top of the noodles, carrot and cucumber. Top the bowls with the cilantro and mint. Pour the sauce over all the bowls and enjoy immediately.

Pork & Marinade

1½ lbs (680 g) pork shoulder

2 tbsp (17 g) minced garlic

2 shallots

2 tbsp (24 g) granulated erythritol

1 tsp black pepper

1 tbsp (15 ml) dark soy sauce

3 tbsp (45 ml) fish sauce

1 tbsp (15 ml) soy sauce

¼ cup (17 g) chopped lemongrass

2 tbsp (30 ml) avocado oil

Sauce

2 tbsp (30 ml) lime juice

2 tbsp (30 ml) fish sauce

2 cloves garlic, minced

2 tbsp (24 g) granulated erythritol

¼ cup (60 ml) warm water

Bowls

16 oz (454 g) tofu shirataki noodles (2 packages)

1 medium carrot, julienned

½ English cucumber, julienned

¼ cup (4 g) cilantro

¼ cup (23 g) mint

6+ Grams Net Carbs   Dairy Free

 Prep time: 30 minutes

 Cook time: 15 minutes

 Serves: 4

Weight: 13.4 oz (380 g) per serving

Net Carbs
 9 g

Protein
49 g

Fat
33 g

552 Calories

 23 g total carbs

 4 g fiber

Roasted Pork Tenderloin with Caraway Sauerkraut

1 g net carbs

A dish with Czech origins, roasted pork tenderloin with caraway sauerkraut is a crowd pleaser and easy to make ahead and portion for future meals. It is simple to prepare, high in protein and full of flavor. Pair with a dish like Radish Au Gratin (page 165) to add healthy fats. You can also serve with sour cream and mustard on the side.

Preheat the oven to 425°F (220°C).

Place the pork in a roasting pan. In a small bowl, mix together the dried dill, onion powder, garlic powder and kosher salt. Sprinkle it over the pork evenly. Bake for 40 to 45 minutes, or until the internal temperature of the pork reaches 165°F (75°C). Allow the pork to rest for 5 minutes before slicing.

While the pork is baking, heat the sauerkraut and caraway seeds in a medium-sized saucepan over medium heat until hot.

Slice the pork thinly and serve on top of a bed of warm sauerkraut.

2 lbs (907 g) pork loin

1 tsp dried dill

1 tsp onion powder

1 tsp garlic powder

2½ tsp (15 g) kosher salt

1 (20-oz [560-g]) jar sauerkraut

2 tsp (4 g) caraway seeds

Paleo

Dairy Free

Prep time:
20 minutes

Cook time:
45 minutes

Serves: 8

Weight: 6 oz (170 g) per serving

Net Carbs
1 g

Protein
33 g

Fat
6 g

210 Calories

4 g total carbs

2 g fiber

Spiced Beef Koftas with Tahini Dipping Sauce

1 g net carbs

Paleo   Dairy Free

These oven-baked koftas are prepared with a blend of aromatic herbs and spices and served with a tahini sauce for dipping. These koftas make for a versatile choice served with salad for lunch or a portion of Zesty Tabbouleh (page 170) or Radish, Cabbage and Sesame Slaw (page 177) for dinner. The koftas can also be batch prepped and frozen or refrigerated for future meals.

Preheat the oven to 400°F (200°C). Soak the wooden skewers in water for 20 minutes.

While the skewers are soaking, prepare the dipping sauce. Crush the garlic and add it to a small mixing bowl. Add the tahini, lemon juice, olive oil, salt and cumin and whisk together until smooth and well combined. Set aside until ready to serve.

Add the ground beef, salt, pepper, ginger, coriander, cumin, cilantro, garlic and lemon zest to a large mixing bowl and combine well with your hands.

Divide the meat into eight equal portions and form into rough sausage shapes with your hands, each roughly 1 inch (3 cm) wide. Thread each of the sausages onto a soaked skewer and arrange them across a shallow baking tray. Transfer the tray to the oven to bake for 16 to 18 minutes, or until golden brown and completely cooked through.

Drizzle the koftas with the tahini dipping sauce and serve with your choice of a keto side.

8 wooden skewers

Tahini Dipping Sauce

1 small clove garlic

1 tsp tahini

1 tsp lemon juice

1 tbsp (15 ml) olive oil

¼ tsp sea salt

¼ tsp ground cumin

Koftas

1 lb (454 g) ground beef

1 tsp sea salt

⅛ tsp pepper

1 tsp ground ginger

1 tsp ground coriander

2 tsp (4 g) ground cumin

1 tbsp (1 g) chopped fresh cilantro

1 clove garlic, minced

1 tsp lemon zest

Prep time:
20 minutes

Cook time:
18 minutes

Serves: 4
(2 skewers each)

Weight: 3.8 oz (108 g)
per serving

Net Carbs
 1 g

Protein
 29 g

Fat
23 g

334
Calories

 2 g total carbs

 1 g fiber

Coriander-Lime Chicken Kebabs with Radish Salad

4 g net carbs

These aromatic, family-friendly chicken kebabs are marinated in zesty lime, fragrant ground cumin and coriander. The crisp and refreshing radish salad makes it a lovely summertime meal. For an easy, light make-ahead dinner or weekday lunch, simply make a batch of the chicken and salad in advance and store in the refrigerator.

Preheat the oven to 400°F (200°C). Soak the wooden skewers in water for 20 minutes.

Crush the garlic and add to a bowl along with the chicken strips, lime juice, lime zest, cumin, coriander, olive oil, salt and pepper. Use your hands to rub the seasonings all over the chicken, then allow the chicken to marinate while the skewers soak.

Thread the tenders onto the soaked skewers, dividing them evenly. Arrange the skewers across a shallow baking sheet and bake for 18 to 20 minutes, or until the chicken is entirely cooked through.

While the chicken is cooking, prepare the salad. Add the radishes, cucumber, onion, cilantro and mint to a serving bowl. Stir together the olive oil, lime juice, syrup (if using), sesame oil, salt and pepper in a small mixing bowl. Drizzle the dressing over the salad and toss to combine. Set aside until the chicken is ready.

Serve the chicken with a portion of salad.

4 wooden skewers

Chicken
2 cloves garlic

22 oz (624 g) chicken tenders, sliced lengthwise into 1-inch (3-cm) strips

2 tsp (10 ml) lime juice

2 tsp (4 g) lime zest

2 tsp (4 g) ground cumin

2 tsp (4 g) ground coriander

2 tbsp (30 ml) olive oil

⅓ tsp sea salt

⅛ tsp black pepper

Salad
40 medium radishes, trimmed and quartered

½ large cucumber, diced in bite-sized chunks

2 tbsp (20 g) red onion, finely diced

2 tbsp (2 g) fresh cilantro, chopped

2 tbsp (11 g) fresh mint, chopped

1 tbsp (15 ml) olive oil

2 tsp (10 ml) lime juice

2 tsp (10 ml) Lakanto maple-flavored syrup (or preferred low-carb sweetener; optional)

2 tsp (10 ml) sesame oil

⅓ tsp sea salt

⅛ tsp black pepper

Paleo   Dairy Free

Prep time:
25 minutes

Cook time:
20 minutes

Serves: 4

Weight: 7 oz (200 g) per serving

Net Carbs
 4 g

Protein
51 g

Fat
18 g

408 Calories

 7 g total carbs

 2 g fiber

Spicy Chicken and Greens

3 g net carbs

Heavily seasoned chicken is flavored with a blend of spices and a bit of cayenne pepper before being cooked to a blackened char. A side of extra buttery vegetables makes this meal truly keto. Cheesy Bread Sticks (page 191) are an excellent accompaniment. Make this recipe ahead as your meal prep for a healthy lunch or dinner.

Butterfly the chicken breasts, slicing all the way through to make four pieces. Season the chicken heavily on the exposed sides with the salt, pepper, paprika, cayenne and onion powder.

Heat the olive oil in a small pan over medium heat. Place the chicken in the olive oil, seasoned side down. Cook the chicken for 4 to 5 minutes per side, so the seasoned side is blackened and the other side is golden brown. Adjust your stove heat as necessary to avoid burning. Set the chicken aside to cool.

Toss the broccoli florets with the olive oil, salt, pepper, Italian seasoning and garlic powder in a large pan. Cook over medium-high heat until the broccoli begins to char.

Turn the heat down to low, and melt the butter into the pan. Stir the fresh spinach into the pan as the butter coats all the vegetables and the spinach wilts. When all the ingredients are heated through, set the pan aside.

Divide the greens among four serving dishes or meal-prep containers. Slice the chicken breasts and arrange with the greens.

Chicken

2 large boneless chicken breasts (about 12 oz [336 g])

½ tsp salt

½ tsp pepper

1 tsp paprika

½ tsp cayenne

¼ tsp onion powder

6 tsp (30 ml) olive oil

Greens

12 oz (336 g) frozen broccoli florets, thawed

4 tsp (20 ml) olive oil

½ tsp salt

½ tsp pepper

1 tsp Italian seasoning

½ tsp garlic powder

4 tbsp (56 g) butter

4 oz (113 g) fresh spinach

30 Minutes or Less

Prep time: 5 minutes

Cook time: 15 minutes

Serves: 4

Weight: 4.1 oz (117 g) per serving

Net Carbs
3 g

Protein
21 g

Fat
26 g

328 Calories

6 g total carbs

4 g fiber

Buffalo Chicken Meatballs with Creamy Blue Cheese Dip

2 g net carbs

In this dish, tender, juicy meatballs are coated with a buttery-hot sauce and then dipped into delicious, cold and creamy dip. Serve with steamed broccoli and sliced raw celery to soak up the extra dip. To make ahead, you can either store the meatballs with the hot sauce in the refrigerator after cooking or freeze the uncooked meatballs on a sheet tray then place in a plastic bag. Add an additional 10 minutes of cooking time if cooking frozen meatballs.

Preheat the oven to 400°F (200°C). Line a baking sheet with parchment paper or a silicone mat.

In a medium-sized bowl, mix the chicken, celery, salt and garlic powder. Use a 1-ounce (28-g) cookie scoop to portion the mixture into sixteen meatballs and place them on the baking sheet. Shape them into meatballs, rolling them between your palms. Bake the meatballs for 20 minutes, or until the internal temperature reaches 165°F (75°C).

While the meatballs are baking, mix the sour cream, blue cheese, mayonnaise and garlic powder in a small bowl and place it in the refrigerator until ready to serve.

Put the butter and hot sauce together in a microwave-safe bowl and melt in the microwave, about 30 to 45 seconds. Toss the hot meatballs in this sauce and then serve with the blue cheese dip.

Meatballs

1 lb (454 g) ground chicken (see Note)

¼ cup (25 g) diced celery

½ tsp kosher salt

¼ tsp garlic powder

Dip

6 tbsp (72 g) sour cream

¼ cup (34 g) crumbled blue cheese

½ cup (120 g) mayonnaise

½ tsp garlic powder

Buffalo Sauce

¼ cup (56 g) salted butter

⅓ cup (80 ml) Frank's RedHot Sauce

Note:

For better texture and flavor, we highly recommend grinding your own chicken in a food processor. Use boneless, skinless chicken thighs and cut into 1-inch (3-cm) chunks, keeping all the fat intact. Freeze on a tray for 15 to 20 minutes and then grind in batches in a food processor until the chicken is fully chopped but not a paste. If you follow this method, you can also chop the celery directly in the food processor and add it to the ground chicken.

 Prep time:
20 minutes (+ 15 minutes if you grind your own chicken)

 Cook time:
20 minutes

Serves: 4

Weight: 5.6 oz (160 g), including meat and dip, per serving

Net Carbs
 2 g

Protein
 23 g

Fat
49 g

519 Calories

 2 g total carbs

 <1 g fiber

Tuna Steaks with Sour Soy Mushrooms

5 g net carbs

This fast make-ahead recipe is simple but full of flavor. Tuna steaks are seared to a medium-rare and are fragrant with garlic and ginger. Mushrooms are simmered in soy sauce and rice vinegar for a play on sweet and sour. You can prepare everything up to 2 days in advance. At your discretion, you can add keto toppings for extra flavor and texture, such as Sriracha and roasted seaweed strips. This is excellent served with Kimchi Fried Cauli-Rice (page 166) or Orange-Ginger Edamame (page 181).

Mix the salt, pepper, garlic powder, onion powder, ginger and sesame seeds together in a small bowl. Rub the seasoning mixture onto both sides of the tuna steaks.

Heat the olive oil in a frying pan over high heat. Place the tuna steaks in the hot oil. The oil should be hot enough that you hear a sizzling sound as they sear. Cook the steaks for 1 to 2 minutes per side. Use a pair of tongs to rotate the tuna steaks in the pan to sear the edges as well. Set the steaks aside to rest and cool.

Return the pan to the stove and turn the heat to low. Add the butter to the pan and scrape with a spatula to loosen any bits of tuna. Add the garlic and ginger to the hot butter and cook until they're fragrant and lightly toasted.

Add the mushrooms, soy sauce and rice vinegar to the pan. Stir and cook over medium-low heat until the mushrooms brown and become tender, 3 to 4 minutes.

Serve the tuna steaks with the mushrooms.

Tuna Steaks

¼ tsp salt

¼ tsp pepper

¼ tsp garlic powder

¼ tsp onion powder

¼ tsp ground ginger

½ tsp sesame seeds

16 oz (454 g) tuna steaks, cut into 4 (4-oz [113-g]) portions

2 tbsp (30 ml) olive oil

Mushrooms

2 tbsp (28 g) butter

1 tbsp (9 g) minced garlic

2 tbsp (20 g) grated ginger root

10 oz (280 g) quartered cremini mushrooms

1 tsp soy sauce

1 tsp rice vinegar

30 Minutes or Less

Prep time: 5 minutes

Cook time: 15 minutes

Serves: 4

Weight: 6.3 oz (178 g) per serving

Net Carbs
5 g

Protein
29 g

Fat
18 g

305 Calories

6 g total carbs

1 g fiber

Garlic Shrimp Zoodles

6 g net carbs

The great thing about this dish is that it's delicious as a hot meal or as cold leftovers, just like takeout. Extra-garlicky shrimp is simmered in a fragrant broth before being served over zucchini "noodles" (aka zoodles). Orange-Ginger Edamame (page 181) is a great accompaniment. If you are avoiding xanthan gum, you can leave it out—it is included as a thickener for the sauce.

Preheat the oven to 400°F (200°C). Line a half-sheet pan (13 x 18 inches [33 x 46 cm]) with parchment paper or lightly spray with cooking spray.

Arrange the spiralized zucchini across the prepared sheet pan in one layer, separating the spirals. Bake for about 15 minutes, until the zucchini is dried out and slightly crispy around the edges. Set the zoodles aside to cool.

While the zucchini is cooking, prepare the shrimp by tossing them in a bowl with the salt, pepper, garlic and olive oil. Arrange the shrimp in a frying pan over medium heat. Place a lid over the shrimp and cook for 2 minutes per side. Use a spoon to transfer the shrimp to a clean bowl and set aside, leaving any excess oil and seasonings in the pan.

Return the pan to a low heat and melt the butter in the pan. Stir in the sesame seeds and green onions and cook until the sesame seeds are toasted and fragrant, 1 to 2 minutes.

Stir the chicken broth, soy sauce and xanthan gum (if using) into the pan. Gently return the shrimp to the pan. Place a lid on the pan and allow the shrimp mixture to cook for another 2 to 3 minutes, just until the sauce thickens and the shrimp is heated through.

For serving, arrange the zoodles in serving dishes. Divide the shrimp and sauce among the bowls. If you desire, you can stir the zoodles in the pan to coat with sauce (off the heat) before serving.

20 oz (560 g) zucchini, spiralized

24 jumbo shrimp, peeled and deveined (about 10 oz [280 g])

½ tsp salt

¼ tsp pepper

2 tbsp (17 g) minced garlic

¼ cup (60 ml) olive oil

2 tbsp (28 g) butter

3 tbsp (28 g) sesame seeds

2 green onions, white and green parts, chopped

½ cup (120 ml) chicken broth

2 tsp (10 ml) soy sauce

1 tsp xanthan gum (optional)

30 Minutes or Less

6+ Grams Net Carbs

Prep time: 10 minutes

Cook time: 15 minutes

Serves: 4

Weight: 4 oz (113 g) per serving

Net Carbs
6 g

Protein
14 g

Fat
24 g

298 Calories

9 g total carbs

3 g fiber

Chili Con Carne

4 g net carbs

The aroma of chili simmering on the stove is one of the great pleasures of life and this large batch is perfect for potlucks, parties or a week's worth of lunches. The base of this chili is made with toasted, pureed guajillo peppers and chiles de árbol. The meat is allowed to simmer on low for several hours until tender and the sauce around the meat has thickened. The fish sauce can be omitted and replaced with salt to taste, but we recommend using it as it adds tremendous flavor.

This chili is a great make-ahead meal as the flavor develops the longer it sits. If you plan to keep it longer than 4 to 5 days in the refrigerator, we recommend freezing extra servings.

Serve each bowl with crumbled cotija cheese, black olives, diced avocado and sour cream. If you cannot find cotija cheese, which is a salty white Mexican cheese that looks similar to feta, feel free to substitute cheddar, pepper Jack or your favorite cheese.

Prep time:
20 minutes

Cook time:
3 hours 25 minutes

Serves: 20

Weight: 4 oz (113 g) per serving

Net Carbs
4 g

Protein
18 g

Fat
23 g

302 Calories

6 g total carbs

2 g fiber

Toast the guajillo peppers and chiles de árbol in a dry frying pan over medium-high heat until fragrant. Do not allow them to smoke. This should only take 1 to 2 minutes total.

Place the toasted chilies in a microwave-safe bowl and cover them with half of the beef stock. Cover with plastic wrap and microwave for 5 minutes. Carefully remove the stems from the chilies and puree them with the stock using a stick blender. Set aside.

Cut the beef into 1-inch (3-cm) chunks and sprinkle the chunks with the salt.

In a large heavy-bottomed pot, add the avocado oil and heat the pot until very hot over medium-high heat. Add the diced beef in batches to the pot, making sure there is only a single layer of beef at a time to ensure the best sear. Allow the beef to cook on one side for 3 to 4 minutes, until nicely seared. Stir and cook for another 3 to 4 minutes, until the other side has browned. Remove the seared beef to a bowl. Repeat with the remaining beef until all the meat is seared.

(continued)

5 dried guajillo peppers

5 dried chiles de árbol

1 qt (946 ml) beef stock, divided

2¾ lbs (1.25 kg) beef chuck roast

1 tsp kosher salt

2 tbsp (30 ml) avocado oil

½ small white onion, diced

4 cloves garlic, minced

½ tsp cinnamon

2 tsp (5 g) cumin seeds

¼ tsp allspice

2 tsp (1 g) dried oregano

2 tbsp (30 ml) fish sauce

2 tbsp (30 ml) apple cider vinegar

1 cup (242 g) crushed tomatoes

10 tbsp (83 g) crumbled cotija cheese

10 tbsp (100 g) black olives

2 avocadoes, diced

10 tbsp (120 g) sour cream

Chili Con Carne (continued)

Add all the seared beef back into the pot along with the onion and garlic. Cook, stirring, for 1 to 2 minutes.

Add in the rest of the beef stock, the chile puree, the cinnamon, cumin, allspice, oregano, fish sauce, vinegar and tomatoes. Allow the mixture to simmer on low for 2½ to 3 hours, or until the meat is very tender and the liquid around the meat has thickened slightly.

Top each bowl with cotija cheese, olives, avocados and sour cream. Serve hot.

Keto Coach Says:

Get familiar with spices and use them with everything! Spices and herbs such as cumin, turmeric, cinnamon, allspice, chilies, garlic, basil, thyme and oregano offer a host of benefits from improving digestive health to reducing inflammation. They add almost no carbs but pack a ton of flavor.

Pepperoni Pizza

6 g net carbs

You don't have to miss pizza while on a diet—you can have the best of both worlds! This is our version of the Internet-popular Fathead Pizza Dough. This pizza is topped with marinara sauce, pepperoni, fresh basil and fresh mozzarella. Like any pizza, you can add your own favorite toppings, but you can keep this pizza dough recipe in your back pocket for life.

To make this recipe more than 5 days in advance, you can freeze balls of dough and allow them to defrost in the refrigerator overnight. The texture of the pizza dough will be slightly more crumbly than pizza dough that was not frozen. You can also precook the pizza dough after the initial rest in the refrigerator by baking it for 22 minutes. Allow it to cool, then wrap and freeze. When baking, allow the prebaked crust to defrost for at least a few hours, top as desired and bake.

The day before you want to make your pizza, make the dough. In a large mixing bowl, mix together the almond flour and the egg until you have a lump-free paste.

Combine the shredded mozzarella and cream cheese in a small pot over low heat. Melt the cheeses, stirring often. You can use a lid to trap heat in the pot, but make sure you check the cheese frequently to avoid burning. It should take just 3 to 5 minutes to melt and stir the cheeses into a smooth, consistent blend.

Let the cheese cool for about 30 seconds. Then, mix it into the almond flour paste. Take your time to fully incorporate the ingredients into a dough (it will be very sticky). When the cheese is cool enough, you can use your hands to knead the dough. Scrape the finished dough into plastic wrap, and wrap the dough tightly (you can also use the plastic to help you finalize the kneading).

Let the dough chill overnight, or for at least 12 hours, in the refrigerator.

(continued)

Dough

1¼ cups (120 g) almond flour

1 large egg

12 oz (336 g) shredded mozzarella

4 oz (113 g) cream cheese

6+ Grams
Net Carbs

Prep time:
15 minutes + 12 hours
chill time

Cook time:
30 minutes

Serves: 6

Weight: 3.8 oz (107 g)
per serving

Net Carbs
6 g

Protein
24 g

Fat
39 g

475
Calories

9 g total carbs

3 g fiber

Pepperoni Pizza (continued)

The day you're ready to make your pizza, preheat the oven to 375°F (190°C). On a large piece of parchment paper, roll the dough out into a large disc about ½ inch (13 mm) thick. You can use additional almond flour to dust your surface for rolling (simply brush it away when done). When your dough is rolled out, transfer it to a pizza baking tray (see Note), leaving it on the parchment paper. Use a fork to poke a series of holes through the center of the dough (this prevents shrinking in the oven).

To assemble the pizza, spread the marinara sauce across the dough, leaving 1 to 2 inches (3 to 5 cm) of the outside edge of the crust bare. Top with slices of pepperoni, chopped fresh basil and the mozzarella balls.

Bake the pizza for about 27 minutes. Look for the same signs as you would baking a regular pizza—bubbling cheese and a golden brown crust. Slice the pizza into six pieces for serving.

Note:

If you do not have a large round dish for baking your pizza, you can also bake on a rectangular sheet tray—just roll your dough into the appropriate shape.

Pizza

¼ cup (63 g) marinara

1 oz (28 g) pepperoni

6 leaves fresh basil, chopped

12 pieces (4.5 oz [122 g]) mozzarella ciliegine, halved

Slow Cooker Stuffed Peppers

7 g net carbs

These slow-cooked peppers are stuffed with ground beef, melty grated cheese and aromatic spices and are topped with cooling sour cream to serve.

These are great to prep in advance and simply throw in the crock pot to slow cook. They are perfect served with a simple side salad dressed with Creamy Citrus-Avocado Dressing (page 147).

Slice the bell peppers in half lengthwise and scoop out the core and seeds. Arrange the bell peppers in the base of a slow cooker.

Add the ground beef, cheddar cheese, paprika, cumin, coriander, oregano, chili powder, garlic powder, tomato sauce, salt and pepper to a large mixing bowl. Add the green onions and mix again until well combined.

Divide the beef mixture evenly between the bell pepper halves, packing the mixture in tightly.

Cover the slow cooker with the lid, and cook on high for 2½ hours or until the peppers are soft and tender and the beef is cooked through.

Top with sour cream and a scattering of fresh cilantro to serve.

2 medium red bell peppers

14 oz (400 g) ground beef

1½ cups (170 g) grated cheddar cheese

1 tsp smoked paprika

1 tsp ground cumin

1 tsp ground coriander

1 tsp dried oregano

1 tsp chili powder

1 tsp garlic powder

½ cup (120 ml) tomato sauce

¼ tsp sea salt

⅛ tsp black pepper

2 large green onions, thinly sliced

¼ cup (48 g) sour cream

1 tbsp (1 g) fresh cilantro

6+ Grams
Net Carbs

Prep time:
15 minutes

Cook time:
2½ hours

Serves: 4

Weight: 4 oz (113 g) per serving

Net Carbs
7 g

Protein
38 g

Fat
29 g

455
Calories

10 g total carbs

3 g fiber

hearty salads & soups

One of the most common misconceptions about keto is that it involves eating bacon and steak for every meal. Though bacon and steak have their place at the table, the backbone of a good keto diet is made of tons of low-carb vegetables and healthy fats. Soups and salads are perfect ways to add both to your diet, plus they are an easy way to make a quick lunch or round out a main course meal as a side.

We've included one of my favorites from the Carb Manager recipe database: the Superfood Keto Salad (page 132). I could happily eat this salad every day for lunch, plus it is vegan and dairy free, so it can work as a side dish for people who have restrictive diets. The Deluxe Taco Salad (page 139) has a delightful twist on the typical tortilla bowl and the Cream of Cauliflower Soup (page 148) is quick, easy and scales and reheats well, making it perfect to make in a batch for the week. Any of the soups go very well with Buttermilk Biscuits (page 158), Garlic-Herb Bread (page 161) or Cheesy Bread Sticks (page 191).

We've also included several recipes for keto salad dressings, which are great to have on hand to whip up a quick salad. If you have one of these dressings, a bag or box of pre-washed greens, some toasted nuts and an avocado, a lunch or side salad can be on the table in less than 5 minutes.

nuts for nuts (and seeds!)

Adding a handful of nuts to a simple green salad or a soup helps add healthy fats to your diet while also adding crunch and flavor.

Here are some common nuts/seeds and grams of net carbs and fat per tablespoon:

Almonds:
1 g net carbs, 4 g fat

Cashews:
2 g net carbs, 4 g fat

Walnuts:
1 g net carbs, 5 g fat

Pecans:
<1 g net carbs, 4 g fat

Peanuts:
1 g net carbs, 5 g fat

Pistachios:
1 g net carbs, 3 g fat

Pine nuts:
1 g net carbs, 6 g fat

Macadamia nuts:
<1 g net carbs, 6 g fat

Brazil nuts:
<1 g net carbs, 6 g fat

Pumpkin seeds:
1 g net carbs, 4 g fat

Sesame seeds:
1 g net carbs, 4 g fat

Sunflower seeds:
1 g net carbs, 4 g fat

Superfood Keto Salad

4 g net carbs

This superfood salad is a powerhouse of nutrition, packed with healthy, raw, low-carb veggies and a hearty dose of plant-based fats and protein. Naturally vegan friendly, this salad makes a great lunch, a hearty side salad or a versatile potluck dish. To make the salad up to 5 days in advance, proceed as directed but add the avocado right before serving.

Add the spinach and broccolini to a large mixing bowl.

Add the garlic to a small mixing bowl with the olive oil, tahini, lime juice and a pinch of salt. Stir well to combine.

Add the avocado to the bowl with the broccolini and spinach. Season with a little salt and toss to combine.

Sprinkle the pumpkin seeds and hemp seeds over the salad, stirring them into the vegetables.

Pour the tahini dressing over the salad and mix thoroughly, coating all the vegetables.

Let the salad stand for 10 minutes before serving to allow the flavors to blend.

4 cups (120 g) baby spinach

2 cups (144 g) chopped broccolini, tough ends removed and cut into bite-size pieces

2 cloves garlic, minced

2 tbsp (30 ml) olive oil

2 tbsp (30 g) tahini

2 tbsp (30 ml) lime juice (from one whole lime)

¼ tsp + a pinch of salt

1 medium avocado, diced

½ cup (65 g) hulled pumpkin seeds

½ cup (80 g) hemp seed heads

Dairy Free   30 Minutes or Less

Vegetarian   Paleo

 Prep time:
10 minutes + 10 minutes to rest

Cook time:
None

Serves: 4

Weight: 4 oz (113 g) per serving

Net Carbs
4 g

Protein
15 g

Fat
34 g

 387 Calories

 11 g total carbs

 7 g fiber

Gado-Gado Salad

5 g net carbs

This keto take on an Indonesian gado-gado salad is packed with crisp and crunchy low-carb veggies and healthy fats and is drizzled in a spicy and tangy peanut dressing. This is a perfect lunch for sharing, served on a large platter.

Add the lime juice, sesame oil, peanut butter, tamari, olive oil, garlic powder and chili flakes to a small mixing bowl. Whisk together until smooth.

Add the green beans to a small pan of boiling water and simmer for 4 to 5 minutes until fork tender. Drain and rinse immediately under cold water to refresh. Pat dry.

Heat the sesame oil in a skillet over medium heat and add the bean sprouts and green beans. Stir-fry for 4 to 5 minutes until the bean sprouts are cooked through.

Arrange the hard-boiled eggs in a large serving dish along with the avocado, shrimp, bell pepper, cucumber, radishes, green beans and bean sprouts. Drizzle everything with the dressing and scatter with chopped fresh cilantro to serve.

To make ahead, prepare all components except the avocado and sliced egg and keep covered in the refrigerator for up to 2 days. Add the avocado and egg and drizzle with dressing just before serving.

Dressing

2 tsp (10 ml) lime juice

2 tsp (10 ml) sesame oil

2 tsp (10 g) unsalted peanut butter

2 tbsp (30 ml) tamari sauce

1 tbsp (15 ml) olive oil

½ tsp garlic powder

1 tsp dried chili flakes

Salad

2.4 oz (70 g) green beans

2 tbsp (30 ml) sesame oil

2.4 oz (70 g) bean sprouts

4 medium hard-boiled eggs, sliced

1 avocado, thinly sliced

5 oz (142 g) cooked jumbo shrimp

½ medium red bell pepper, thinly sliced

3 oz (85 g) cucumber, sliced into batons about ½ inch (13 mm) thick and 2½ inches (7 cm) long

4 medium radishes, thinly sliced

2 tbsp (2 g) fresh cilantro

30 Minutes or Less   Dairy Free   Paleo

 Prep time: 15 minutes

 Cook time: 10 minutes

Serves: 4

Weight: 6.6 oz (187 g) per serving

Net Carbs
 5 g

Protein
17 g

Fat
24 g

 314 Calories

 10 g total carbs

 4 g fiber

Steak Arugula Salad

5 g net carbs

This dish is full of iron, calcium and many other wonderful nutrients. It is all topped with an apple cider–garlic vinaigrette. It's a showstopper! If possible, season the steak with salt an hour ahead of time and allow it to rest at room temperature to get a really good sear. The salad can be prepared up to 3 days in advance—just add the avocado and dressing right before serving.

Season the steak with salt and let it rest at room temperature for up to 1 hour.

Heat a small, nonstick sauté pan over medium-high heat. Add the oil and heat until shimmering. Add the steak and cook on the first side for 4 to 5 minutes. Flip and cook on the other side for 2 to 3 minutes. This will bring the steak close to medium-rare, depending on thickness. Cook for a minute or so longer for a well-done steak. Let the steak rest for 5 to 10 minutes.

While the steak is resting, make the dressing. Whisk together the olive oil, vinegar, salt, pepper and garlic to emulsify.

Arrange the arugula, avocados, cucumber and tomatoes on a platter. Slice the steak into thin strips and place on top of the arugula. Drizzle the vinaigrette over the salad.

Salad

24 oz (680 g) tip sirloin steak (or other preferred cut)

1 tsp kosher salt

2 tbsp (30 ml) extra-virgin olive oil

6 cups (120 g) arugula

2 avocados, sliced

1 large English cucumber, peeled and sliced

12 cherry tomatoes

Dressing

4 tbsp (60 ml) extra-virgin olive oil

4 tbsp (60 ml) apple cider vinegar

1 tsp kosher salt

½ tsp black pepper

2 cloves garlic, grated

Make It New:

There are many varieties of arugula available. Rocket has spiky leaves and a peppery, nutty flavor; Astro has smooth leaves and a milder flavor. Experiment to see which type you like best—all types are low in carbs and packed with nutrients, especially vitamin K. You can substitute baby kale or spinach if you don't like arugula's spicy flavor.

  Dairy Free Paleo

 Prep time: 20 minutes

 Cook time: 10 minutes

 Serves: 4

Weight: 6.6 oz (187 g) per serving

Net Carbs
5 g

Protein
54 g

Fat
46 g

 668 Calories

 13 g total carbs

 7 g fiber

Deluxe Taco Salad

5 g net carb

A taco salad never feels complete unless it's served in a large, crunchy taco shell. Here's the next best thing: a keto tortilla shell made of cheddar cheese. Cheddar "taco shells" are filled with seasoned ground beef, avocado and tomatoes. As the shell breaks apart and mixes with the tangy lettuce, it tastes just like a traditional taco salad, maybe even better!

Evenly arrange ½ cup (56 g) of the shredded cheddar in a small nonstick pan. Make sure the cheese isn't clumped up in any areas. Heat the cheese over low heat, undisturbed. Let the cheese melt, bubble and cook to a dark orange color (about 3 minutes). Use a spatula to reshape the edges of the tortilla as needed.

Find a bowl whose base is a similar shape to the taco shell you want to make, and turn the bowl upside down. Take the pan off the heat and drain the excess grease off the cheese. Use a spatula to transfer the tortilla over the base of the bowl. Shape the tortilla's edges over the bowl as it hardens. If the cheese is too soft and breaks apart, it needs to be cooked longer. Repeat these steps for the remaining three taco shells.

While the taco shells are setting, combine the ground beef, olive oil, salt, pepper, cumin, paprika, onion powder and red pepper flakes in a frying pan over medium heat. Cook the beef, stirring occasionally, until it's golden brown and crispy. Set aside.

For the dressing, whisk together the mayonnaise, lime juice, salt, garlic and cilantro. Toss the chopped lettuce with the dressing.

Separate the dressed lettuce between four serving dishes. Set a hardened taco shell in the center of each plate of lettuce. Fill each shell with its share of ground beef. Make sure the beef has cooled enough that it doesn't melt your cheese tortilla. Arrange the diced tomato and avocado on top of the beef. Add any additional salad garnishes or toppings you desire, such as hot sauce, salsa or sour cream.

Taco Shell

2 cups (226 g) cheddar cheese, shredded

Beef

16 oz (454 g) ground beef, 90% lean

4 tsp (20 ml) olive oil

½ tsp salt

½ tsp pepper

½ tsp cumin

1 tsp paprika

½ tsp onion powder

½ tsp red pepper flakes

Dressing

6 tbsp (83 g) mayonnaise

8 tsp (40 ml) lime juice

¼ tsp salt

1 tsp garlic, minced

2 tbsp (2 g) minced cilantro

Salad

8 oz (227 g) chopped lettuce mix

3 oz (85 g) grape tomatoes, diced

6 oz (170 g) avocado, diced

Hot sauce, for topping (optional)

Salsa, for topping (optional)

Sour cream, for topping (optional)

30 Minutes or Less

Prep time: 10 minutes

Cook time: 20 minutes

Serves: 4

Weight: 6.6 oz (187 g) per serving

Net Carbs
5 g

Protein
45 g

Fat
58 g

743 Calories

10 g total carbs

5 g fiber

Tuna and Kale Salad

4 g net carbs

Dairy Free   30 Minutes or Less   Paleo

This simple keto salad is rich with healthy fats and low-carb veggies. The salty capers and aromatic fresh basil contrast with the slightly bitter note of the chicory. If you make a batch of Cheesy Bread Sticks (page 191), try breaking a few and adding them to this salad as a crouton substitute.

This makes a light and tasty lunch for four, perfect for mid-week work lunches and meal prepping. You can make this salad up to 5 days in advance. The sturdy greens can be dressed ahead of time, but, if possible, add the avocado at the last minute.

 Prep time:
22 minutes (including standing time)

 Cook time:
None

 Serves: 4

Add the chicory to a large serving bowl with the baby kale, tomatoes, olives, avocado and capers. Toss well to combine.

Drain the tuna and flake it into the salad. Season with black pepper and stir again to combine.

Add the basil to a small mixing bowl along with the lemon juice and olive oil. Mix to combine and drizzle over the salad. Let stand for 10 minutes before serving.

Salad

2 small heads red chicory, ends and core removed

4 cups (260 g) baby kale

8 cherry tomatoes, quartered

20 Kalamata olives, thinly sliced

1 large avocado, diced

2 tsp (6 g) baby capers

5 oz (142 g) canned tuna

⅛ tsp black pepper

Dressing

2 tbsp (6 g) finely chopped fresh basil

2 tbsp (30 ml) lemon juice

4 tbsp (60 ml) extra-virgin olive oil

Weight: 6.6 oz (187 g) per serving

Net Carbs
 4 g

Protein
12 g

Fat
25 g

313 Calories

Make It New:

If you can't find chicory, any sturdy green, preferably one with a slightly bitter or spicy note, will work. Try endive, arugula, escarole or baby tat soi. Canned sardines make a nice substitution for the tuna.

 17 g total carbs

 13 g fiber

Mixed Berry Poppyseed Vinaigrette

2 g net carbs

Bright, tart and fruity with beautiful poppyseeds, this dressing is a crowd-pleaser and absolutely stunning over lettuce greens. It goes very well with salads that include toasted walnuts or ricotta cheese. The salad dressing keeps in the refrigerator for at least a week.

Add the olive oil, vinegar, mixed berries, salt and pepper to a small blender or a blender cup and blend until emulsified. Stir in the poppyseeds until well combined. Serve over salad greens of your choice. Store in a small jar. If the dressing separates, shake well until emulsified again.

¼ cup (60 ml) extra-virgin olive oil

¼ cup (60 ml) white wine vinegar

½ cup (93 g) frozen mixed berries, thawed

1 tsp kosher salt

⅛ tsp black pepper

1 tsp poppyseeds

Keto Coach Says:

Berries are not only delicious, they are also high in antioxidants, low in carbohydrates and have a good amount of fiber. This makes them the perfect keto fruit! Add them to your smoothies, eat as an easy dessert or top your keto waffles and pancakes with them.

Dairy Free

30 Minutes or Less

Vegetarian

Paleo

Prep time: 8 minutes

Cook time: None

Serves: 4

Weight: 1.8 oz (50 g) per serving

Net Carbs
2 g

Protein
<1 g

Fat
14 g

137 Calories

3 g total carbs

1 g fiber

Herbs de Provence Apple Cider Vinaigrette

<1 g net carbs

This pungent, herby vinaigrette will be great over any type of mixed green salad or even a slaw-style salad. It is full of delicious extra-virgin olive oil, herbs de Provence and apple cider vinegar. Leftover roast pork is perfect with this dressing. The dressing keeps well in the refrigerator for up to 2 weeks.

Mix the herbs de Provence, garlic, mustard, salt, pepper and apple cider vinegar in a small bowl. Add the oil slowly, whisking very well until the dressing has emulsified. Store in a small jar in the refrigerator and shake before using until emulsified if the dressing has separated.

1 tsp herbs de Provence

1 clove garlic, grated

1 tsp Dijon mustard

1 tsp kosher salt

⅛ tsp black pepper

¼ cup (60 ml) apple cider vinegar

¼ cup (60 ml) extra-virgin olive oil

Dairy Free | 30 Minutes or Less

Vegetarian | Paleo

Prep time: 8 minutes

Cook time: None

Serves: 4

Weight: 1 oz (28 g) per serving

Net Carbs
<1 g

Protein
<1 g

Fat
14 g

125 Calories

<1 g total carbs

<1 g fiber

Creamy Citrus-Avocado Dressing

2 g net carbs

Fresh avocado makes for an ultra-creamy dressing or dip. In this dressing, avocado is paired with bright citrus flavors and seasoned with garlic and black pepper. The preparation is simple, yet bold, and works great with endive, little gem lettuce or any crunchy, slightly bitter green. For a perfect match, try adding seafood or bacon as a garnish. This salad dressing will store well in the refrigerator for up to 5 days.

Add the avocado oil, lime juice, garlic, salt, pepper and avocado to a small blender or a blender cup and blend with a stick blender until creamy. Store in a small jar in the refrigerator until ready to use.

6 tbsp (90 ml) avocado oil

2 tbsp (30 ml) lime juice

2 tbsp (30 ml) lemon juice

1 clove garlic

1 tsp kosher salt

⅛ tsp black pepper

1 small avocado

Dairy Free

30 Minutes or Less

Vegetarian

Paleo

Prep time:
8 minutes

Cook time:
None

Serves: 4

Weight: 1.7 oz (48 g) per serving

Net Carbs
2 g

Protein
<1 g

Fat
22 g

206
Calories

3 g total carbs

1 g fiber

Cream of Cauliflower Soup

6 g net carbs

Delicious, sweet cauliflower is sautéed with diced onions and celery, simmered gently with heavy cream and pureed to smooth perfection. The key to allowing the soup's flavor to develop properly is to be sure not to brown the onions and celery, but to sweat them instead. This means cooking them on a lower heat until they are translucent. Using frozen cauliflower rice is very convenient and recommended. If your blender has a soup setting, use it for a silky texture.

Heat a medium-sized stockpot over medium-high. When the pot is hot, add the oil and let it heat until shimmering. Add the onion and celery and turn the heat down to medium. Stir and cook until the vegetables are translucent, 3 to 4 minutes. Add the kosher salt and stir well.

Add the cauliflower rice and cook until fully defrosted if using frozen and slightly translucent if using fresh. Then add the heavy cream and water. Bring the mixture to a gentle boil.

As soon as it comes to a boil, place the hot mixture into a blender and blend on high until very smooth. If your blender has a soup setting, use that to puree. Taste the soup, adding more salt to taste.

Place the pine nuts and sunflower seeds in a dry, small, nonstick sauté pan. Heat over medium heat and toast the nuts until browned, about 1 to 2 minutes. Mix in the chia seeds and parsley.

Divide the soup between four bowls and top with the toasted nut topping.

To make ahead, keep in the refrigerator for up to 5 days or freeze in individual portions for longer storage. The nut topping can be kept refrigerated in an airtight container for up to a week, or frozen.

Soup

1 tbsp (15 ml) extra-virgin olive oil

½ cup (80 g) diced white onion

¼ cup (25 g) diced celery

¼ tsp kosher salt

3½ cups (400 g) fresh or frozen cauliflower rice

1 cup (240 ml) heavy cream

1 cup (240 ml) water

Topping

2 tsp (5 g) pine nuts

1 tsp sunflower seeds

⅛ tsp chia seeds

1 tsp fresh parsley, finely minced

30 Minutes or Less

6+ Grams Net Carbs

Prep time:
10 minutes

Cook time:
20 minutes

Serves: 4

Weight: 8.1 oz (231 g) per serving

Net Carbs
6 g

Protein
5 g

Fat
28 g

304 Calories

11 g total carbs

5 g fiber

Shrimp Noodles with Coconut Broth

5 g net carbs

Dairy Free

30 Minutes or Less

Paleo

These deliciously fragrant zucchini "noodles" are cooked in an aromatic coconut broth infused with dried and fresh spices and herbs and topped with juicy pan-fried shrimp. This is a comforting warm lunch or light dinner option.

Prep time: 10 minutes

Cook time: 15 minutes

Serves: 4

Slice the ends off the zucchini and peel away the outer skin, discarding the peel. Peel the zucchini flesh into long ribbons and set aside. If you would like thinner noodles, slice the long ribbons in thirds lengthwise.

Heat ½ tablespoon (7 g) of the coconut oil in a large casserole dish over low-medium heat. Add the ginger, garlic and green onions and sweat for 1 or 2 minutes, until tender and fragrant.

Add the turmeric, cumin, coriander and lime juice. Stir well and cook for an additional minute.

Add the coconut milk and vegetable stock and stir well. Bring the mixture to a gentle boil, then reduce the heat and simmer for 6 to 7 minutes.

While the broth is cooking, heat the remaining coconut oil in a skillet over medium heat. Add the jumbo shrimp and season with the salt and pepper. Cook the shrimp until they turn pink and are piping hot through.

Add the zucchini noodles to the broth and cook for 1 minute, or until tender.

Divide the soup among four serving bowls and top each with the cooked shrimp and oil and the cilantro to serve.

1 large zucchini

1 tbsp (14 g) coconut oil, divided

1 (1-inch [3-cm]) piece fresh ginger, grated

1 clove garlic, crushed

2 small green onions, thinly sliced

1 tsp ground turmeric

1 tsp ground cumin

1 tsp ground coriander

1 tsp lime juice

⅔ cup (160 ml) coconut milk

4 cups (960 ml) vegetable stock

12 oz (340 g) raw jumbo shrimp

⅛ tsp salt

⅛ tsp black pepper

1 tbsp (1 g) fresh cilantro, chopped

Weight: 10 oz (280 g) per serving

Net Carbs
 5 g

Protein
 22 g

Fat
12 g

216 Calories

7 g total carbs

2 g fiber

Make It Fast:

Use premade or purchased zucchini spirals. Trader Joe's is a good place to find them if they are not available in your local supermarket.

Watercress Soup with Feta Cheese

5 g net carbs

30 Minutes or Less

Vegetarian

This wholesome watercress soup is loaded with healthy low-carb vegetables and blended until velvety smooth. Watercress adds a peppery note, but arugula or spinach can be substituted instead. The soup is served with a crumbling of tangy feta cheese and toasted pine nuts for added texture. Serve with Garlic-Herb Bread (page 161).

This is also a superb option for batch cooking, as you can prepare the soup in bulk and freeze individual serving-sized portions. Simply thaw and reheat thoroughly, then top with fresh cheese and pine nuts to serve.

Add the pine nuts to a dry skillet over medium-low heat and toast gently for 2 to 3 minutes, until lightly golden. Transfer to a small plate or bowl and let cool.

Melt the butter in a large saucepan or casserole dish over medium-low heat. Add the shallot to the pan, sweating gently until tender.

Add the zucchini to the pan along with the lemon zest, thyme and nutmeg. Stir well to combine and cook for 1 or 2 minutes to soften.

Add the vegetable stock and bring it to a boil. Reduce the heat to medium and simmer for 5 minutes, until the zucchini is tender.

Add the watercress and stir well. Simmer for 1 to 2 minutes more, until the leaves are just wilted.

Transfer the soup to a blender or use a hand-held stick blender and process until completely smooth. Strain the soup if there are still visible chunks. Add salt to taste.

Divide the soup among four bowls and crumble the feta and pine nuts over the top to serve.

Store in the refrigerator for up to 5 days. The pine nuts taste best if toasted right before serving.

1 tbsp (8 g) pine nuts

1½ tbsp (20 g) butter

½ medium shallot, thinly sliced

1 medium zucchini, peeled and sliced into ½-inch (13-mm)-thick discs

1 tsp lemon zest

1 tsp fresh thyme

¼ tsp ground nutmeg

4 cups (960 ml) vegetable stock

2½ cups (85 g) watercress

Salt, to taste

½ cup (75 g) feta cheese

Prep time: 12 minutes

Cook time: 15 minutes

Serves: 4

Weight: 6.9 oz (196 g) per serving

Net Carbs
 5 g

Protein
5 g

Fat
 13 g

160 Calories

 6 g total carbs

 1 g fiber

Italian Meatball Soup

5 g net carbs

This simple meatball soup is packed with flavor from aromatic fresh basil and dried oregano and combined with tender zucchini noodles to serve.

This makes a hearty and warming lunch or dinner option served on its own or with Garlic-Herb Bread (page 161) for dipping. For batch cooking, you can prepare the meatballs in advance and freeze. Increase the cooking time to 15 minutes after adding the meatballs if they are added frozen.

Slice the ends off the zucchini and peel off the outer skin, discarding the skin. Peel the zucchini flesh into long ribbons and set aside.

Add the ground turkey and beef to a large mixing bowl. Add the garlic, oregano, salt and pepper. Use your hands to combine all the ingredients thoroughly, then divide the mixture into 24 equal portions, rolling them into small meatballs. Set to one side.

Heat the oil in a large saucepan or casserole dish over low-medium heat. Add the onion and celery and cook gently for 3 to 4 minutes until tender.

Add the vegetable stock and bring to a boil.

Add the meatballs carefully to the pan, reduce the heat to medium and simmer for 10 minutes.

Add the zucchini noodles and basil and cook for an additional 2 minutes, until the zucchini and meatballs are completely cooked through. Scatter with extra fresh basil to serve.

1 large zucchini

9 oz (255 g) ground turkey

9 oz (255 g) ground beef

1 clove garlic, crushed

2 tsp (2 g) dried oregano

¼ tsp sea salt

⅛ tsp black pepper

1 tbsp (15 ml) olive oil

½ large white onion, finely diced

1 large celery stalk, thinly sliced

4½ cups (1 L) vegetable stock

¼ cup (6 g) fresh basil, plus more for garnish

Dairy Free

30 Minutes or Less

Paleo

Prep time: 12 minutes

Cook time: 17 minutes

Serves: 4

Weight: 8 oz (227 g) per serving

Net Carbs
5 g

Protein
34 g

Fat
25 g

392 Calories

7 g total carbs

1 g fiber

satisfying sides

Do you ever miss the feeling of biting into a perfectly flaky biscuit, slathered with butter? Do you dream of rich scalloped potatoes or a take-out container of fried rice? If you miss starchy sides like bread, noodles or baked potatoes, the recipes in this chapter will help you stick with your keto diet. We've also included a number of vegetable sides to round out your main course meals.

Stocking your freezer with riced cauliflower and frozen edamame and keeping radishes, zucchini, shirataki noodles and almond meal in the fridge will help these sides come together in a snap.

Other keto-friendly vegetables include asparagus, bitter melon, bamboo shoots, bok choy, broccoli, Brussels sprouts, cabbage, celery, chard, cucumbers, fennel, green beans, eggplant, jicama, kale, kohlrabi, mushrooms, mustard greens, okra, peppers, spinach and salad greens. All these vegetables, paired with a keto-friendly fat (try a Compound Butter from page 183), make an excellent side dish for any meal.

make your own cauliflower rice

To make your own cauliflower rice, wash and dry a head of cauliflower, then cut it into large chunks, including the stem.

Blitz in a food processor in batches until the cauliflower is in small bits, similar to tiny grains of rice. Spread onto a sheet pan lined with parchment paper and freeze, then transfer to a plastic freezer bag. This will keep the cauliflower rice from sticking together in one giant chunk.

If you do not have a food processor, you can use a sharp knife to mince the cauliflower in batches instead.

Buttermilk Biscuits

5 g net carbs

These biscuits make great sides or breakfast items. They are made with almond flour and buttermilk, which keeps them moist and fluffy. Serve them warm from the oven with salted butter or slice open and layer with your favorite sandwich topping. The combo of Chicken-Fried Steak Cutlets (page 89), pickled peppers and mayonnaise makes a stupendous sandwich.

Preheat the oven to 375°F (190°C). Line a sheet tray with parchment paper or a silicone mat.

Whisk the eggs, coconut oil, buttermilk and kosher salt together in a medium bowl. Make sure you use solid coconut oil. The mixture will look chunky.

In a large bowl, mix the baking powder, baking soda, almond flour and granulated erythritol to combine. Add the egg and milk mixture to the dry ingredients and mix until combined. The texture should be thick enough to scoop, drop on a sheet tray and hold its shape. Using a cookie scoop or two spoons, scoop out the batter in six equal portions and place each scoop on the prepared sheet tray. Shape each biscuit to be round on top because they will not rise in the oven.

Bake for 20 to 25 minutes, until the tops and edges are starting to turn brown and the biscuits are set. Allow the biscuits to cool on the sheet tray until cool enough to handle.

3 eggs

2 tbsp (27 g) coconut oil

¼ cup (60 ml) buttermilk

¼ tsp kosher salt

1 tsp baking powder

1 tsp baking soda

2¼ cups (215 g) almond flour

1 tbsp (12 g) granulated erythritol (Swerve preferred)

Keto Coach Says:

Coconut oil is made up of 60 percent medium chain triglycerides (MCT) oil. MCTs are converted immediately by our liver into ketones, because they cannot be stored. You may add coconut oil to your coffee/tea, dressings and baked goods to increase your body's ketone production.

Vegetarian

Prep time:
12 minutes

Cook time:
25 minutes

Makes 6 biscuits

Weight: 2.3 oz (65 g) per biscuit

Net Carbs
5 g

Protein
12 g

Fat
29 g

328
Calories

11 g total carbs

5 g fiber

Garlic-Herb Bread

3 g net carbs

This bread is perfect for enjoying as a side or snack, but it's even better when used to soak up any keto gravy or sauce you may have with your meal. Allowing the cream cheese and butter to come to room temperature before mixing will help you achieve an even, fluffy texture.

Preheat the oven to 350°F (175°C). Line a 9-inch (23-cm) round pan with parchment paper. If you have a medium loaf pan, you may use this instead.

In a stand mixer, mix the cream cheese and butter until they are smooth and creamy. Scrape down the bowl often with a spatula while mixing.

Slowly mix in the eggs. Again, scrape the bowl down often to achieve a smooth, liquid mixture.

Finally, mix in the almond flour, baking powder, salt, rosemary, thyme and garlic. The batter will be a little loose but thick. Use a spatula to spread the batter into the parchment-lined pan, then smooth the top.

Bake for 35 to 40 minutes, until the loaf is golden brown on top and a wooden toothpick inserted into the center comes out clean.

Allow the bread to cool for 5 minutes before removing from the pan and slicing into eight slices.

4 oz (113 g) cream cheese, softened

8 tbsp (113 g) butter, softened

4 large eggs

1½ cups (145 g) almond flour

1 tsp baking powder

¼ tsp salt

1 tsp dried rosemary

½ tsp dried thyme

2 cloves garlic, minced

Vegetarian

Prep time:
10 minutes

Cook time:
40 minutes

Serves: 8

Weight: 2.4 oz (67 g) per serving

Net Carbs
3 g

Protein
9 g

Fat
30 g

312
Calories

6 g total carbs

2 g fiber

Toasted Sesame Shirataki Noodles

2 g net carbs

These noodles are easy-peasy to make, family-friendly and full of flavor. The tofu shirataki noodles are drained, heated in the microwave and then topped with sesame oil, tamari and rice vinegar. They are very filling and would pair well with any protein, especially those with Asian flavors, like Spicy Korean Short Ribs with Crispy Cabbage (page 93) or Tuna Steaks with Sour Soy Mushrooms (page 118).

Drain the tofu noodles in a strainer, then place them in a microwave-safe bowl. Microwave the noodles on high for 2 minutes. Drain again as more water will be released from the noodles.

Toss the noodles with the tamari, sesame oil and rice vinegar and top with the cilantro and green onion.

2 (8-oz [227-g]) bags tofu shirataki noodles

¼ cup (60 ml) tamari

3 tbsp (45 ml) sesame oil

3 tbsp (45 ml) rice vinegar

¼ cup (4 g) cilantro, chopped

1 green onion, sliced

Make It New:

Add marinara sauce or butter and Parmesan cheese to the noodles after draining for a different flavor profile.

 Vegetarian
 30 Minutes or Less
 Dairy Free

 Prep time: 8 minutes

 Cook time: 2 minutes

 Serves: 4

Weight: 5.5 oz (156 g) per serving

Net Carbs
2 g

Protein
2 g

Fat
11 g

 123 Calories

 4 g total carbs

 2 g fiber

Radish Au Gratin

5 g net carbs

If you are missing potatoes, this dish is your friend. Any type of radish will work, but using mild-flavored Japanese daikon radish will make the dish look and feel very similar to potatoes au gratin. If you use the more common red radish, the tender skin does not need to be peeled. The dish is great served as is, but it is also delicious topped with freshly grated Parmesan cheese and chopped parsley.

Preheat the oven to 375°F (190°C).

Slice the radishes on a mandolin or with a sharp knife in ⅛-inch (3-mm) slices. Place the radishes in a medium-sized saucepan over medium heat and add the cream, garlic, salt and pepper. Bring the mixture to a boil, then take the pan off the heat.

Pour the mixture into a shallow 9 x 13–inch (23 x 33–cm) baking dish. Bake for 25 to 30 minutes, until the radishes are soft and the top is browned.

1 lb (454 g) daikon radish, peeled
1 cup (240 ml) heavy cream
2 cloves garlic, grated or crushed
½ tsp kosher salt
¼ tsp black pepper

Vegetarian

Prep time:
15 minutes

Cook time:
35 minutes

Serves: 4

Weight: 2.5 oz (71 g) per serving

Net Carbs
5 g

Protein
2 g

Fat
22 g

225
Calories

7 g total carbs

2 g fiber

Kimchi Fried Cauli-Rice

3 g net carbs

This fried rice is loaded with flavor and makes a perfect side dish to accompany Spicy Korean Short Ribs with Crispy Cabbage (page 93) or Citrus Salmon (page 61). If you use frozen cauliflower rice, it is an easy last-minute side dish. We are partial to the Chongga Mat Kimchi brand, but any kimchi will work—just check to make sure that the net carbs are less than 4 grams per cup.

Heat a wok over high heat until very hot. Add 1 tablespoon (15 ml) of the avocado oil and swirl the pan to coat the inside surface. Add the ginger and garlic and stir-fry with a spatula for 20 to 30 seconds. Turn down the heat if the garlic starts to brown on the edges.

Add the cauliflower rice and salt and turn the heat down to medium-high. Toss the rice for 3 to 4 minutes, or until it turns lightly golden.

Push the rice to one side of the wok and drizzle the second tablespoon (15 ml) of avocado oil into the cleared area. Crack the egg into the wok in the cleared space. When the white of the egg is almost set, about 1 minute, break up the egg and flip with the spatula. Toss with the rest of the cauliflower.

Add the green onion and kimchi and cook for 1 to 2 minutes, or until the green onion is slightly wilted. Turn off the heat and add the sesame oil. Toss to combine.

2 tbsp (30 ml) avocado oil, divided

1 tbsp (6 g) julienned ginger

2 tsp (6 g) minced garlic

4 cups (455 g) fresh or frozen cauliflower rice

½ tsp salt

1 large egg

1 green onion, sliced on the diagonal

¼ cup (38 g) chopped cabbage kimchi

1 tbsp (15 ml) sesame oil

Dairy Free

30 Minutes or Less

Vegetarian (depending on kimchi)

Paleo

Prep time: 10 minutes

Cook time: 10 minutes

Serves: 4

Weight: 5.4 oz (154 g) per serving

Net Carbs
3 g

Protein
4 g

Fat
12 g

144 Calories

6 g total carbs

3 g fiber

Baked Cauliflower "Mac and Cheese"

6 g net carbs

If you miss mac and cheese, you will love this version with cauliflower. Delicious cauliflower is coated with a keto cheese sauce and then baked to golden perfection. If you or your family are not very excited about eating vegetables, this is a good recipe to try, as the cheese flavor dominates the vegetable flavor.

Preheat the oven to 375°F (190°C). Grease an 8 x 8–inch (20 x 20–cm) baking dish with non-stick cooking spray. Line a baking sheet with paper towels.

Bring a large pot of water to a boil. Blanch the cauliflower florets in the boiling water for 1 minute. Remove the cauliflower with a slotted spoon and place the florets on the paper towel-lined baking sheet. Allow the florets to air dry while you make the cheese sauce.

In a small saucepan, combine the cream cheese and heavy cream. Heat over medium heat, whisking until the cream cheese melts and combines with the cream. Add 1½ cups (168 g) shredded cheese and whisk together until smooth and creamy. Stir in the garlic powder, salt and pepper.

Place the blanched cauliflower in a large mixing bowl and pour the cheese sauce over the top. Fold the mixture together with a spoon, then pour the cheesy cauliflower into the prepared dish. Top with the remaining ½ cup (58 g) of shredded cheese. Bake for 25 minutes, until the top is golden brown and melted.

4 cups (400 g) cauliflower florets, cut into ½-inch (13-mm) chunks

1 oz (28 g) cream cheese

½ cup (120 ml) heavy cream

2 cups (226 g) shredded sharp cheddar cheese, divided

¼ tsp garlic powder

¼ tsp kosher salt

¼ tsp black pepper

6+ Grams Net Carbs Vegetarian

Prep time:
20 minutes

Cook time:
30 minutes

Serves: 4

Weight: 6 oz (170 g) per serving

Net Carbs
6 g

Protein
16 g

Fat
32 g

382
Calories

9 g total carbs

2 g fiber

Zesty Tabbouleh

2 g net carbs

Cauliflower makes an excellent substitution for bulgur wheat in this tabbouleh-inspired side dish. Sumac is a citrusy Middle Eastern spice made from the dried red berries of the sumac bush. If it is not available, you can substitute an additional teaspoon of lemon juice. This side is perfect with Spiced Beef Koftas with Tahini Dipping Sauce (page 110).

Heat a medium-sized pan over medium heat. Add the olive oil. When the oil is hot, add the cauliflower rice and stir occasionally until hot, about 6 to 7 minutes. Turn off the heat and stir in the lemon juice and hot peppers. Transfer the mixture to a bowl to cool slightly.

Add the feta, parsley, herbs, sumac and salt to the cauliflower mixture. Stir well and taste. Adjust the seasonings by adding additional salt or lemon juice to taste. Chill for at least 30 minutes before serving.

2 tbsp (30 ml) olive oil

10 oz (280 g) fresh or frozen cauliflower rice

2 tsp (10 ml) lemon juice, plus more to taste

1 tsp pickled peppers, minced (we recommend Mama Lil's Hot brand)

1 oz (28 g) feta, diced in ¼-inch (6-mm) cubes

½ cup (30 g) chopped parsley

¼ cup (15 g) chopped additional fresh herbs—can include mint, thyme, oregano, green onion, chives, sorrel, etc.

½ tsp sumac

½ tsp salt, plus more to taste

Vegetarian

Prep time:
15 minutes

Cook time:
10 minutes
+ 30 minutes to chill

Serves: 4

Weight: 3.5 oz (100 g) per serving

Net Carbs
 2 g

Protein
 3 g

Fat
 9 g

102
Calories

5 g total carbs

3 g fiber

Zucchini Fries with Curry Mayo Dipping Sauce

6 g net carbs

The zucchini is not the star of the show in this recipe (although it is coated in crispy goodness); the star is the curry mayo dipping sauce. Not only is the sauce highly flavorful, but it's creamy, tangy and super keto-friendly. Feel free to make the sauce in advance, store it in the refrigerator and heat it up any time you want to snack on zucchini fries, avocado slices or seasoned mixed vegetables.

Preheat the oven to 425°F (220°C). Line a sheet tray with parchment paper.

Cut the zucchini into fries about 1 x 3 inches (3 x 8 cm) each. Use paper towels to press the excess moisture out of the zucchini fries, without squishing them.

In a small bowl, whisk the egg white. On a plate, mix together the almond flour, Parmesan, salt, pepper, onion powder, garlic powder and paprika.

One by one, dip the zucchini fries in the egg whites, let any excess drip off, then roll the fry in the almond flour breading. Arrange each breaded zucchini fry on the parchment-lined sheet tray.

Bake the fries for 35 to 40 minutes, until golden brown and crisp on the outside. Flip the fries over about halfway through the baking process. Let the fries cool for 5 minutes before transferring to a serving dish.

To make the curry mayo, whisk the mayonnaise, lemon juice, curry powder, turmeric, paprika and salt in a glass or microwave-safe bowl. Heat the bowl for 15 seconds in the microwave for a warm, smooth dipping sauce.

Serve the zucchini fries with the sauce.

Fries

20 oz (560 g) zucchini (about 3 medium zucchini)

1 egg white

½ cup + 2 tbsp (70 g) almond flour

½ cup (56 g) Parmesan cheese, grated

¼ tsp salt

½ tsp pepper

½ tsp onion powder

½ tsp garlic powder

1 tsp paprika

Curry Mayo

6 tbsp (83 g) mayonnaise

2 tsp (10 ml) lemon juice

½ tsp curry powder

¼ tsp turmeric

⅛ tsp paprika

⅛ tsp salt

6+ Grams Net Carbs

Vegetarian

Prep time: 15 minutes

Cook time: 40 minutes

Serves: 4 (6–7 fries + 2 tbsp [30 ml] sauce per serving)

Weight: 3.5 oz (100 g) per serving

Net Carbs
6 g

Protein
12 g

Fat
29 g

331 Calories

10 g total carbs

4 g fiber

Sheet Pan Zucchini

3 g net carbs

Zucchini is a staple in keto side dishes. Thin-sliced zucchini is layered with loads of herbs and spices and fresh lemon zest for a zing of citrus. This dish is perfect in the summer when zucchini is in season and works well with any small summer squash.

Preheat the oven to 375°F (190°C). Spray a 9 x 13–inch (23 x 33–cm) sheet tray with non-stick cooking spray.

Slice the zucchini into ¼-inch (6-mm) slices. In a large mixing bowl, toss the zucchini with the salt, pepper, oregano, rosemary, garlic, lemon zest and olive oil.

Arrange the zucchini slices across the sheet tray, overlapping each piece halfway over the last. Scrape any excess seasonings out of the mixing bowl and drizzle over the zucchini.

Bake the zucchini for 35 minutes, or until the zucchini is puckered and golden brown.

1 lb (454 g) zucchini (about 2 medium)

½ tsp salt

½ tsp pepper

1 tsp dried oregano

½ tsp dried rosemary

2 garlic cloves, crushed

½ tsp lemon zest

1½ tbsp (22 ml) olive oil

 Dairy Free Vegetarian Paleo

 Prep time: 10 minutes

 Cook time: 35 minutes

 Serves: 4

Weight: 3.5 oz (100 g) per serving

Net Carbs
3 g

Protein
2 g

Fat
5 g

 68 Calories

 5 g total carbs

 1 g fiber

Radish, Cabbage and Sesame Slaw

2 g net carbs

This vibrant radish slaw is packed with low-carb veggies and aromatic cilantro and coated in a rich sesame mayonnaise. This is a quick and easy side dish, perfect for accompanying Asian-inspired dishes or your choice of protein.

Add the sesame seeds to a dry skillet over low-medium heat and toast gently while shaking the pan or stirring with a spoon for 2 to 3 minutes, until lightly golden. Set aside.

Add the cabbage, radishes, green onions, cucumber and cilantro to a mixing bowl and stir well.

In a separate small bowl, add the tahini, lime juice, sesame oil, mayonnaise, tamari sauce, garlic powder and pepper. Beat together, then add the water, a little at a time, stirring until smooth and creamy.

Spoon the dressing over the vegetables and mix well, coating everything in the mayonnaise.

Scatter the toasted sesame seeds over the salad and stir through to serve.

1 tsp sesame seeds

⅔ cup (60 g) red cabbage, finely sliced

8 medium radishes, finely sliced

2 medium green onions, finely sliced

¼ large cucumber, sliced into narrow 1-inch (3-cm) strips

1 tbsp (1 g) fresh cilantro, roughly chopped

1 tsp tahini

1 tsp lime juice

1 tsp sesame oil

1½ tsp (7 g) mayonnaise

1½ tsp (8 ml) tamari sauce

¼ tsp garlic powder

⅛ tsp black pepper

1 tbsp (15 ml) water

Dairy Free

30 Minutes or Less

Vegetarian

Paleo

 Prep time:
15 minutes

 Cook time:
3 minutes

 Serves: 4

Weight: 2 oz (57 g) per serving

Net Carbs
 2 g

Protein
1 g

Fat
3 g

46 Calories

 3 g total carbs

 1 g fiber

Seaweed Salad

2 g net carbs

This is a perfect crowd-pleasing keto side: nutrient-dense seaweed in a sweet sesame vinegar dressing. Many recipes use sugar to tame the acidity of the vinegar. The maple sweetener in this recipe is sugar free and blends with the toasted sesame seeds and sesame oil to give the salad a subtle sweet flavor. You can also substitute 1 teaspoon of erythritol or omit the sweetener entirely. The salad stores well in the refrigerator for several days.

Rehydrate the dried wakame by placing it in a bowl and covering it with cold water. Set aside for at least 15 minutes.

Mix the cucumber slices with ½ teaspoon salt in a medium bowl and set aside.

To make the dressing, whisk together the rice vinegar, maple-flavored syrup, sesame oil, soy sauce and the remaining ¼ teaspoon of salt.

Toast the sesame seeds in a small pan over medium heat, stirring constantly until you hear them pop and they start to turn golden brown.

Drain the wakame and add it to a serving bowl. Add the cucumber, dressing, onion and carrot. Sprinkle the toasted sesame seeds on top.

¼ cup (7 g) dried wakame

1 medium cucumber, peeled and sliced ⅛ inch (3 mm) thick

¾ tsp salt, divided

2 tbsp (30 ml) rice vinegar

1 tbsp (15 ml) Lakanto maple-flavored syrup (or preferred low-carb sweetener)

2 tsp (10 ml) sesame oil

1 tsp soy sauce

2 tsp (6 g) sesame seeds

¼ yellow onion, thinly sliced

1 tbsp (6 g) shredded carrot

30 Minutes or Less

Vegetarian

Prep time:
20 minutes

Cook time:
5 minutes

Serves: 4

Weight: 3.5 oz (100 g) per serving

Net Carbs
2 g

Protein
1 g

Fat
3 g

60 Calories

6 g total carbs

2 g fiber

Orange-Ginger Edamame

5 g net carbs

This is a quick and easy snack or side dish. A hint of orange contrasts with the nutty flavor of tamari. This recipe makes enough for a dinner side dish plus extra for snacks.

Place the frozen edamame in a microwave-safe bowl. Cover with plastic wrap and microwave until hot, for 3 to 4 minutes on high.

Mix the orange zest, ginger, avocado oil and tamari in a small bowl and pour the mixture over the hot edamame. Sprinkle with the kosher salt. Mix well and serve hot or chill in the refrigerator for a snack.

1 (14-oz [397-g]) bag frozen, shell-on edamame

2 tsp (4 g) orange zest

1 tsp grated ginger

1 tbsp (15 ml) avocado oil

2 tbsp (30 ml) tamari

¼ tsp kosher salt

30 Minutes or Less   Vegetarian   Dairy Free

 Prep time: 15 minutes

 Cook time: 4 minutes

Serves: 6

Weight: 2.6 oz (75 g) per serving

Net Carbs
 5 g

Protein
8 g

Fat
5 g

 109 Calories

 8 g total carbs

 3 g fiber

Parmesan-Roasted Tomatoes

3 g net carbs

These simple roasted tomato slices are topped with shaved Parmesan, garlic and lemon zest and baked until tender, then topped with fresh basil to serve. These make a quick and easy side to your choice of protein and pairs well with a simple green salad.

Preheat the oven to 400°F (200°C) and line a shallow baking tray with parchment paper.

Slice each tomato into four even slices.

Arrange the tomato slices across the parchment-lined baking tray. Crush the garlic and sprinkle it over the tomatoes along with the lemon zest, salt and pepper and top with the shaved Parmesan. Drizzle the olive oil over the tomatoes.

Transfer to the oven to bake for 10 to 12 minutes, or until the tomatoes are tender and the Parmesan is golden.

Scatter with the basil to serve.

*See image on page 156.

4 small tomatoes

1 clove garlic

1 tsp lemon zest

¼ tsp sea salt

⅛ tsp black pepper

2 tbsp (14 g) shaved Parmesan

1½ tbsp (22 ml) olive oil

2 tbsp (5 g) fresh basil, chopped

30 Minutes or Less   Vegetarian

Prep time:
5 minutes

Cook time:
12 minutes

Serves: 4

Weight: 4.1 oz (116 g) per serving

Net Carbs
3 g

Protein
2 g

Fat
6 g

77
Calories

4 g total carbs

1 g fiber

Compound Butters

<1 g net carbs

Compound butters are a great way to add flavor (and fat) to all sorts of dishes. They work well paired with roasted chicken, fish, grilled steak, keto bread, cauliflower rice or vegetables. The options are limitless and so are the flavor variations. Here are three of our favorites.

Spicy Spanish Compound Butter

<1 g net carbs

In a medium-sized bowl, using a fork or small spatula, mix the butter, olives, salt, garlic, thyme, orange zest and crushed red pepper well.

Place the butter mixture on a piece of plastic wrap and wrap it into a log. Chill the butter in the refrigerator until firm, about 30 minutes. When ready to serve, slice into individual portions. For a quick Spanish rice, mix a bag of frozen cauliflower rice with a batch of this butter.

½ cup (113 g) butter, at room temperature

6 Kalamata olives, chopped

⅛ tsp kosher salt

1 clove garlic, minced

6 sprigs fresh thyme, leaves only

½ tsp orange zest

½ tsp crushed red pepper

(continued)

Prep time:
8 minutes + 30 minutes chill time

Cook time:
None

Serves: 8

Weight: 0.7 oz (20 g) per serving

Net Carbs
<1 g

Protein
<1 g

Fat
12 g

109 Calories

<1 g total carbs

<1 g fiber

Herby Italian Garlic-Parm Compound Butter

<1 g net carbs

In a medium-sized bowl, using a fork or small spatula, mix the butter, garlic, Parmesan, Italian seasoning and salt well.

Place the butter mixture on a piece of plastic wrap and wrap into a log. Chill in the refrigerator until firm, about 30 minutes. When ready to serve, slice into individual portions. Try this butter melted into spinach for an easy side dish.

½ cup (113 g) butter, at room temperature

2 cloves garlic, grated

3 tbsp (22 g) freshly grated Parmesan

1 tsp dried Italian seasoning

⅛ tsp kosher salt

Rosemary–Blue Cheese–Black Pepper Compound Butter

<1 g net carbs

In a medium-sized bowl, using a fork or small spatula, mix the butter, blue cheese, pepper, rosemary, thyme and salt well.

Place the butter mixture on a piece of plastic wrap and wrap into a log. Chill in the refrigerator until firm, about 30 minutes. When ready to serve, slice into individual portions. This butter is perfect melted onto a rib-eye steak for a luxurious treat.

½ cup (113 g) butter, at room temperature

3 tbsp (26 g) crumbled blue cheese

¼ tsp freshly cracked black pepper

1½ tsp (1 g) chopped fresh rosemary

3 sprigs fresh thyme, leaves only

⅛ tsp kosher salt

Keto Coach Says:

Butter is one of the best dietary sources of butyric acid. Butyric acid is a short-chain fatty acid that the good bacteria in our colon use for energy. This may help reduce inflammation in our gut, which may improve our gut health and digestion.

Net Carbs
<1 g

Protein
1 g

Fat
12 g

114 Calories

<1 g total carbs

<1 g fiber

Net Carbs
<1 g

Protein
1 g

Fat
12 g

114 Calories

<1 g total carbs

<1 g fiber

Herby Italian Garlic-Parm

Rosemary–Blue Cheese–Black Pepper

savory snacks

Having an array of ready-to-go snacks at your fingertips can be lifesaving when you first start eating keto. We recommend choosing at least one snack a week to make ahead and have on hand.

Several of these recipes can also double as appetizers for a party—Salsa Cheese Party Dip (page 196) is loved by everyone, keto or not, and Pizza Trail Mix (page 188) and Cheesy Bread Sticks (page 191) are fun and festive. Fried Mozzarella (page 204) also makes a great salad topping.

There are also many quick and easy snacks that are great to have on hand that do not even need a recipe, like hard-boiled eggs, pickles, avocados, cheese slices, cut up celery and cucumber, mixed nuts, pork rinds, olives, deli meat, sausages and canned fish and seafood, such as smoked sardines.

spice up your eggs

Hard-boiled eggs are the perfect keto snack: One large egg has 1 gram net carbs, 5 grams fat, 6 grams protein and 78 calories.

I follow the 6 minute/10 minute formula for eggs: Boil water in a large pot. Add whole eggs and start a timer: 6 minutes for runny soft boiled eggs and 10 minutes for hard boiled. You can adjust according to your preference; for example, my son likes a 7-minute egg with a creamy yolk. Stir the eggs gently a few times during the first 2 to 3 minutes of boiling. When the timer goes off, remove the eggs with a slotted spoon and chill under cold running water. I use a pencil to mark the eggs after they have boiled—an O for soft boiled and an X for hard boiled. Store in the refrigerator for up to 1 week.

I love hard-boiled eggs dipped in olive oil mixed with Trader Joe's Everything But the Bagel seasoning. I also peel hard-boiled eggs under running water and add them to the juice that is left over in a jar of pickles—within 1 day the eggs take on a delicious pickled flavor. A little drizzle of toasted sesame oil plus a sprinkle of chili flakes and salt over chilled soft-boiled eggs sliced in half is also delicious.

Pizza Trail Mix

5 g net carbs

A savory trail mix is a refreshing change from the typical sweet flavors, and this crunchy version totally tastes like pizza! If you're craving those flavors, this is a handy keto snack option to have on hand throughout the week. The nut mixture can be stored in an airtight container and the chorizo simply added when ready to serve.

Preheat the oven to 300°F (150°C) and line a shallow baking tray with parchment paper.

Add the almonds, walnuts and pine nuts to a mixing bowl along with the oregano, basil, garlic powder, salt, pepper and rosemary. Drizzle the syrup and oil over the mixture and use your hands to rub the seasonings and syrup all over the nuts and seeds.

Arrange the seasoned nut mixture in an even layer across the parchment-lined baking tray. Transfer to the oven to bake for 15 minutes or until golden, turning halfway through. Set aside to cool completely.

Return the cooled nuts to a mixing bowl. Add the sun-dried tomatoes and toss to combine. Store in an airtight container until ready to serve.

When ready to serve, add the chorizo to the bowl, stirring until evenly distributed throughout the nut mixture.

¾ cup (110 g) almonds

½ cup (60 g) walnuts

¼ cup (35 g) pine nuts

1 tsp dried oregano

½ tsp dried basil

¼ tsp garlic powder

¼ tsp salt

⅛ tsp black pepper

1 tsp fresh rosemary, finely chopped

1 tsp Lakanto maple-flavored syrup (or preferred low-carb sweetener; optional)

½ tbsp (8 ml) olive oil

1 tbsp (2 g) sun-dried tomatoes (dry packed, not in oil), roughly chopped

1 tbsp (15 g) cured, ready-to-eat chorizo, finely diced

Dairy Free

Prep time:
13 minutes

Cook time:
15 minutes + 30 minutes cooling time

Serves: 4

Weight: 1.6 oz (45 g) per serving

Net Carbs
5 g

Protein
10 g

Fat
32 g

344
Calories

10 g total carbs

5 g fiber

Cheesy Bread Sticks

2 g net carbs

These keto dough sticks are rich with Parmesan cheese and baked until soft and doughy in the center with a slightly crisp and golden exterior. These make a crowd-pleasing sharing snack for families or parties—perfect for holidays and gatherings. They also make an excellent salad topping in place of croutons.

Preheat the oven to 300°F (150°C) and line a large, shallow baking tray with parchment paper.

Add the almond flour, Parmesan, oregano, salt and pepper to a food processor. Blend well to combine, forming a crumb consistency.

Roughly dice the butter and add it to the food processor. Blend again until well combined.

With the motor of the food processor running, slowly add 3 tablespoons (45 ml) of the cold water, a little at a time, blending until a dough forms. Wrap the dough in parchment paper and transfer it to the refrigerator to chill for 10 minutes.

Unwrap the chilled dough and break it into fifteen even-sized portions, roughly the size of ping pong balls. Arrange the dough balls on the parchment-lined baking tray and use your hands to gently roll each ball into a long sausage shape, roughly ½ inch (13 mm) wide and 6 inches (15 cm) long.

Beat the egg with the remaining 1 tablespoon (15 ml) of water and brush liberally all over the dough sticks. Transfer the baking tray to the oven to bake for 35 minutes, until golden brown and firm to the touch. Set aside to cool a little and firm up before serving.

2 cups (190 g) almond flour

⅔ cup (65 g) grated Parmesan

1 tbsp (3 g) dried oregano

1 tsp salt

¼ tsp black pepper

⅓ cup (75 g) unsalted butter

4 tbsp (60 ml) cold water, divided

1 egg

Vegetarian

Prep time:
25 minutes (including chill time)

Cook time:
35 minutes

Makes 15
bread sticks

Weight: 0.8 oz (23 g)
per bread stick

Net Carbs
2 g

Protein
5 g

Fat
13 g

146
Calories

3 g total carbs

2 g fiber

Cheddar Zucchini Crisps

4 g net carbs

Not only are these cheddar zucchini crisps great as a snack to tide you over until your next meal, but they add a satisfying salty crunch paired alongside a protein or a main course. You can easily double or triple this recipe to have enough snacks for the week.

Preheat the oven to 425°F (220°C). Line a sheet tray with parchment paper.

Use a grater to shred the zucchini into fine shreds. Spread the zucchini on the parchment-lined sheet. Bake for 25 to 30 minutes to dry out the zucchini, tossing the zucchini every 10 minutes. You'll have a mix of green and golden brown pieces.

Remove the sheet tray from the oven but leave the oven on. Allow the zucchini shreds to cool until you can touch them. In a bowl, combine the zucchini shreds with the shredded cheddar cheese (make sure the zucchini isn't too warm—it should not melt the cheese).

Use a tablespoon to arrange 10 spoonfuls of the mix on a sheet tray (you can use the same parchment paper as before). Spread each portion out to create a thin disk.

Bake for an additional 10 minutes. The zucchini will turn golden brown and crisp while the cheddar will melt and "glue" the crisps in place.

Allow the crisps to cool for 1 to 2 minutes before transferring with a spatula to a plate. Store in an airtight container.

10 oz (280 g) zucchini (1 large zucchini)

6 tbsp (42 g) shredded cheddar cheese

Vegetarian

Prep time:
8 minutes

Cook time:
40 minutes

Serves: 2
(5 crisps per serving)

Weight: 1.2 oz (33 g) per serving

Net Carbs
4 g

Protein
7 g

Fat
8 g

110 Calories

5 g total carbs

1 g fiber

Prosciutto Chips

0 g net carbs

You won't miss potato chips after you make these prosciutto chips. Perfect for a solo snack or a party treat with a keto dip—like the Salsa Cheese Party Dip (page 196) or the guacamole from Guacamole Parmesan Cups (page 200)—prosciutto chips make the best finger food! Curb your craving for something salty and crunchy with no regrets.

Preheat the oven to 375°F (190°C). Line a sheet tray with parchment paper.

Cut the six slices of prosciutto into four rectangles each, totaling 24 pieces. Arrange the pieces on the parchment-lined sheet tray.

Bake the prosciutto for 10 minutes. Keep an eye on the prosciutto during the last 1 to 2 minutes to avoid burning.

Remove the tray from the oven and allow the prosciutto to cool and become crispy. Enjoy with your favorite low-carb dip!

6 slices prosciutto

30 Minutes or Less   Dairy Free   Paleo

 Prep time:
4 minutes

 Cook time:
10 minutes

 Serves: 4
(6 pieces per serving)

Weight: 0.5 oz (13 g) per serving

Net Carbs
0 g

Protein
3 g

Fat
1 g

 25 Calories

 0 g total carbs

 0 g fiber

Salsa Cheese Party Dip

4 g net carbs

This simple yet flavorful dip combines oozy melted cheese and a simple tomato salsa, blended together until rich and creamy. This is a sure-to-please sharing dip option for families and parties that even non-keto friends can enjoy.

Heat the olive oil in a small pan over medium-low heat and add the tomatoes, red onion, chili pepper, cumin and garlic powder. Cook gently for 2 to 3 minutes, until softened and fragrant.

Add the cream cheese to the pan and stir until melted and combined. Season with the salt and pepper.

Add the grated cheese and stir until hot, melted and well combined.

Serve with your choice of low-carb crudités, such as bell pepper strips, jicama, and sliced cucumber or Prosciutto Chips (page 195).

1 tbsp (15 ml) olive oil

6 cherry tomatoes, finely diced

¼ small red onion, finely diced

½ small red chili pepper, finely diced

½ tsp ground cumin

½ tsp garlic powder

½ cup (120 g) cream cheese, softened

¼ tsp sea salt

⅛ tsp black pepper

1 cup (113 g) grated cheddar

30 Minutes or Less   Vegetarian

 Prep time:
10 minutes

 Cook time:
10 minutes

 Serves: 4

Weight: 1.8 oz (50 g) per serving

Net Carbs
4 g

Protein
9 g

Fat
22 g

244
Calories

 4 g total carbs

 1 g fiber

Curried Deviled Eggs

1 g net carbs

These quick and easy deviled eggs are rich with aromatic curry, fresh cilantro, creamy mayonnaise and a hint of lime. These make an excellent starter, snack or potluck dish, perfect to grab and go between meals.

Using a teaspoon, gently scoop the yolk from each egg and add the yolks to a mixing bowl along with the mayonnaise, mustard, curry powder, lime juice, salt, pepper and cilantro. Use a fork to mash everything together, then mix thoroughly until smooth and well combined.

Divide the mixture evenly between the hollowed eggs, filling each space where the yolk was.

Scatter the green onion over the eggs to garnish.

4 hard-boiled eggs, peeled and sliced in half lengthwise

1 tbsp (15 g) mayonnaise

½ tsp mustard

1 tsp curry powder

1 tsp lime juice

¼ tsp sea salt

⅛ tsp black pepper

1 tbsp (1 g) fresh cilantro, finely chopped

1 large green onion, thinly sliced

Dairy Free 30 Minutes or Less

Vegetarian Paleo

Prep time:
15 minutes

Cook time:
None

Serves: 4
(2 halves per serving)

Weight: 1.95 oz (55 g) per serving

Net Carbs
 1 g

Protein
 6 g

Fat
7 g

96 Calories

 1 g total carbs

 0 g fiber

Guacamole Parmesan Cups

3 g net carbs

30 Minutes or Less   Vegetarian

Cheese is a wonder-food of the keto diet. It can take so many shapes and has so many textures, and in this case it serves as its own snack-sized cup. Each cup made of Parmesan cheese is filled with a quick, made-from-scratch guacamole. Once you learn this technique, making cheese cups is quick and easy—try using 1 tablespoon (5 g) of Parmesan and mini-muffin tins for a one-bite appetizer shell and fill with spoonfuls of salad, cooked shrimp or roast chicken mixed with a bit of mayonnaise.

 Prep time:
10 minutes

 Cook time:
10 minutes

Preheat the oven to 350°F (175°C). Line a sheet tray with parchment paper or a silicone baking sheet.

Arrange 2 tablespoons (10 g) of Parmesan in eight portions on the parchment-lined tray, spreading each portion out into a thin circle.

Bake the cheese for 6 to 8 minutes. Watch for the cheese to melt, bubble and obtain crispy edges. When the circles are crisp on the outside and just a little soft in the centers, remove the tray from the oven. Use a spatula to transfer each Parmesan circle to a clean muffin tin. Press the Parmesan circles gently into the tins as they harden to form cups. Set the tray of Parmesan cups aside to cool.

In a mixing bowl, use a fork to smash together the avocado, lime juice, cilantro, salt, onion powder and garlic powder into a guacamole.

Carefully set the cooled, firm Parmesan cups on a serving plate. Spoon an even portion of guacamole into each cup and garnish each cup with a cherry tomato half.

16 tbsp (80 g) Parmesan, shredded

10 oz (280 g) avocado

1 tbsp (15 ml) lime juice

¼ cup (4 g) cilantro, chopped

¼ tsp salt

¼ tsp onion powder

¼ tsp garlic powder

4 small cherry tomatoes, sliced in half

 Serves: 4
(2 cups per serving)

Weight: 3.2 oz (90 g)
per serving

Net Carbs
 3 g

Protein
12 g

Fat
18 g

233
Calories

 8 g total carbs

 5 g fiber

BLT Chicken Snack Cups

1 g net carbs

This snack tastes just like a mini bacon, lettuce and tomato sandwich! Fresh iceberg lettuce, juicy tomatoes, melted cheddar and the perfect amount of crispy bacon come together for a tasty little snack or party appetizer. Pop this easy finger food into your mouth without worrying about carbs. The lettuce wilts slightly in the oven, but the flavors merge in a delightful way. If you prefer crispy lettuce, add it at the end.

Preheat the oven to 350°F (175°C). Spray a six-cup muffin tin with pan spray. Line each tin with a slice of chicken. Top the chicken with equal amounts of the lettuce, then the tomatoes. Arrange about ½ tablespoon (4 g) of shredded cheddar in each chicken cup, followed by 1 teaspoon of bacon bits.

Bake the cups for 15 minutes. Allow the cups to cool for a few minutes before enjoying. These can be stored in the refrigerator for up to 3 days.

6 slices deli chicken

¾ cup (54 g) shredded iceberg lettuce

6 grape tomatoes, diced

3 tbsp (21 g) shredded cheddar cheese

2 tbsp (14 g) bacon bits

30 Minutes or Less

Prep time:
10 minutes

Cook time:
15 minutes

Makes 6 snack cups

Weight: 1.1 oz (32 g) per snack cup

Net Carbs
 1 g

Protein
 5 g

Fat
4 g

65
Calories

2 g total carbs

<1 g fiber

Fried Mozzarella

5 g net carbs

30 Minutes or Less · Vegetarian

These easy, deliciously tender mozzarella discs are breaded in almond flour and Italian seasoning then pan fried until crisp and golden. These are tasty as the base for a lunchtime salad or served as a snack with your favorite low-carb dipping sauce. If you eat tomatoes, a simple marinara sauce is a satisfying match.

Beat the egg in a shallow bowl. In a second shallow bowl, mix the almond flour, Italian seasoning, salt and pepper.

Dip each slice of mozzarella in the beaten egg, then dredge in the seasoned almond flour until well coated all over with a generous layer of breading.

Heat the olive oil in a large skillet over medium-high heat. When the oil is hot, add two of the breaded mozzarella discs and cook for 1 to 1½ minutes on each side, until the breading is golden. Repeat with the remaining two discs, adding more oil as needed. Alternatively, if you have a large enough skillet, you can cook all four at the same time.

1 medium egg

1 cup (96 g) almond flour

1 tbsp (3 g) Italian seasoning

⅛ tsp sea salt

⅛ tsp black pepper

1 (10.5-oz [298-g]) ball of mozzarella, sliced into 4 equal discs about ½ inch (13 mm) thick

1 tbsp (15 ml) olive oil, plus more if needed

Prep time:
8 minutes

Cook time:
7 minutes

Makes 4 slices

Weight: 1.7 oz (48 g) per slice

Net Carbs
5 g

Protein
23 g

Fat
37 g

446 Calories

8 g total carbs

3 g fiber

Meat and Cheese Rolls

These are very easy to make and are a great help with menu planning if you are short on calories but near the limit on carbs. They also work well on an appetizer tray for a party or premade in the refrigerator to round out a keto-friendly lunch. The flavor varieties are endless as you can use any type of cheese stick and any type of cured meat.

Mozzarella Cheese and Salami Rolls

2 g net carbs

Wrap two slices of salami around one cheese stick. Repeat with the remaining cheese sticks. Keep chilled until serving.

8 medium slices (3.2 oz [90 g]) salami

4 sticks (4 oz [113 g]) mozzarella cheese

(continued)

30 Minutes
or Less

Prep time:
5 minutes

Cook time:
None

Makes 4 rolls

Weight: 1.7 oz (48 g)
per roll

Net Carbs
 2 g

Protein
11 g

Fat
12 g

159
Calories

 2 g total carbs

 0 g fiber

Roast Beef and Pepper Jack Rolls

<1 g net carbs

Wrap one slice of roast beef around each cheese stick. Keep chilled until ready to serve.

4 (1.4-oz [40-g]) slices natural roast beef

4 (3-oz [85-g]) pepper Jack cheese sticks

Weight: 1 oz (28 g) per roll

Net Carbs

<1 g

Protein
6 g

Fat
7 g

89 Calories

<1 g total carbs

0 g fiber

Rotisserie Chicken and Sharp Cheddar Rolls

<1 g total carbs

Wrap one slice of rotisserie chicken around each cheddar cheese sick. Keep chilled until ready to serve.

4 (1.5-oz [42-g]) slices deli rotisserie chicken

4 (3-oz [85-g]) sharp cheddar cheese sticks

Weight: 1 oz (28 g) per roll

Net Carbs

<1 g

Protein
7 g

Fat
7 g

102 Calories

<1 g total carbs

0 g fiber

Roast Beef and Pepper Jack   Rotisserie Chicken and Sharp Cheddar

Cucumber, Egg and Lox Bites

2 g net carbs

This recipe is enjoyable as a snack, a light breakfast or an appetizer. Refreshing cucumber is the base for layers of tangy cream cheese, hard-boiled egg and smoky lox. A sprig of dill and a dash of Tabasco adds a lively zing.

Boil the eggs for 10 minutes for hard-boiled eggs (see page 187). After cooling in ice water, peel the eggs and slice each into four slices, resulting in twelve slices of egg. Set aside.

Press the cucumber slices between two paper towels to soak up excess water. Arrange the cucumber slices on a serving plate.

Warm the cream cheese for 10 to 15 seconds in the microwave to soften. Spread a shmear of cream cheese across each cucumber slice. Press a slice of hard-boiled egg on top of the cheese, then add a slice of lox. Sprinkle a pinch of pepper over each portion.

Garnish with dill and a dash of Tabasco sauce, if desired.

3 eggs

1 (4-oz [113-g]) cucumber, sliced into 12 pieces, about ½ inch (13 mm) thick

1 oz (28 g) cream cheese

1.5 oz (42 g) cold-smoked salmon (lox), sliced into 12 pieces

¼ tsp pepper

A few sprigs of fresh dill

Tabasco sauce (optional)

30 Minutes
or Less

Prep time:
15 minutes

Cook time:
12 minutes

Serves: 4
(3 bites per serving)

Weight: 3 oz (85 g)
per serving

Net Carbs
2 g

Protein
7 g

Fat
7 g

100
Calories

2 g total carbs

<1 g fiber

Greek Mini Skewers

1 g net carbs

Your snack could not get easier with this recipe. Simply lift and slide right into your mouth. These would make a good snack between meals but are also easy enough to make in large quantities for gatherings. This is a nice recipe to use as a template for other quick-to-prepare snacks—meat, diced cheese or any pickle works well.

Stack one piece of feta, olive, basil and grape tomato on each toothpick, for a total of 12 mini skewers. Store in an airtight container in the refrigerator.

2.75 oz (77 g) feta cheese, cut into 12 pieces

12 pitted green olives

3 large basil leaves, torn or sliced into 4 pieces each

12 grape tomatoes

30 Minutes or Less   Vegetarian

 Prep time: 5 minutes

 Cook time: None

Serves: 4 (3 toothpicks per serving)

Weight: 3 oz (85 g) per serving

Net Carbs
 1 g

Protein
3 g

Fat
6 g

71 Calories

 2 g total carbs

 1 g fiber

Sesame Feta with Tahini Dip

4 g net carbs

This crisp and tender feta cheese is coated in a sweet tahini sauce, rolled in crunchy sesame seeds, then grilled until golden. This makes a great snack or base for a salad served with a portion of sweet tahini sauce for dipping.

Add the tahini, olive oil, lemon juice, syrup, pepper and garlic powder to a mixing bowl. Whisk together until smooth.

Cut the feta into sixteen equal-sized cubes. Place the sesame seeds in a shallow dish or plate.

Pour one-third of the tahini mixture into a small bowl to use as a dipping sauce. Gently toss the feta chunks in the rest of the tahini sauce. Roll the tahini-coated feta in the sesame seeds so that they are well covered.

Heat the broiler to high. Arrange the feta cubes across a shallow grill tray and broil for 1 to 2 minutes on each side or until lightly golden all over—enough to brown the seeds but not so much that the cheese will melt. Allow the feta to cool slightly, then serve with the remaining tahini sauce for dipping.

2 tsp (10 g) tahini

2 tsp (10 ml) olive oil

2 tsp (10 ml) lemon juice

2 tsp (10 ml) Lakanto maple-flavored syrup (see Note)

⅛ tsp black pepper

¼ tsp garlic powder

7 oz (200 g) feta cheese

⅓ cup (45 g) sesame seeds

Note:

If you are avoiding all sweeteners, you may omit the Lakanto maple-flavored syrup, which will reduce the total carbs by 1 gram and the calories by 2 calories per serving.

30 Minutes or Less   Vegetarian

 Prep time: 12 minutes

 Cook time: 8 minutes

 Serves: 4

Weight: 1.9 oz (54 g) per serving

Net Carbs
4 g

Protein
9 g

Fat
19 g

229 Calories

 7 g total carbs

 2 g fiber

sweets & fat bombs

Many people find that their desire for sweets diminishes the longer they stay keto—and that even a single strawberry can taste sweet and satisfying, reducing the need for artificial sweeteners. But if you still have a sweet tooth, eating keto doesn't have to mean depriving yourself of treats and sweets. During the transition period, these recipes can help you bridge the gap—providing a touch of sweetness without a ton of carbs.

We have included recipes for fat bombs that can double as truffle- or fudge-like desserts, as well as traditional cakes, crumbles and ice creams that are sweetened with erythritol, monk fruit or stevia. There are also two recipes that require no sweetener at all: Pine Nut Biscotti (page 231) and Almond Panna Cotta (page 239).

keto sweetener tips

If you choose to use sweeteners, we recommend sticking to sugar alcohols like erythritol (or Swerve), monk fruit or stevia as sugar substitutes. Make sure that there is no maltodextrin included as a filler in your sugar substitute, as it is high in carbs.

Some people don't like the flavor of erythritol or stevia, so it can be helpful to experiment to find what works for your taste. Occasionally, sugar alcohols can cause gastric discomfort, so we recommend trying them in small amounts at first, until you know how your body reacts.

Hazelnut Truffle Fat Bombs

1 g net carbs

If you like the flavor of Nutella, these deliciously indulgent fat bombs are not only a decadent treat between meals but are also a decadent way to boost your fats for the day. The texture of the hazelnuts and the crunchy hint of salt are a perfect combination.

Preheat the oven to 350°F (175°C).

Place the whole hazelnuts on a baking tray and bake for 10 minutes, until the nuts are warm and the skin is falling away. If you would like to make your own chopped hazelnuts, add both amounts of hazelnuts to the baking pan, adding slightly less than 6 tablespoons (51 g) of whole hazelnuts to make 6 tablespoons (45 g) of chopped hazelnuts.

Let the nuts cool. When they are cool enough to handle, gently rub the nuts to loosen and remove the skin. It should come away easily.

If you are chopping your own hazelnuts, add slightly less than 6 tablespoons (51 g) of whole toasted hazelnuts to a food processor and process until chopped. Remove from the food processor and place them on a plate.

Transfer ½ cup (68 g) of the toasted hazelnuts to a food processor and blend to a fine crumb. Add the erythritol, cocoa powder, vanilla and salt and blend again to form a thick paste. Add the butter and blend to combine, then add the coconut oil and blend again until smooth and creamy. Spoon the mixture into a freezer-proof container and freeze for 15 to 20 minutes, or until the mixture is firm enough to mold.

Assemble sixteen truffle cases or mini cupcake liners. Scatter the chopped hazelnuts on a plate. Scoop a generous heaped teaspoon of the chilled mixture and roll it into a ball, then roll in the chopped nuts. Place in a truffle case. Repeat until you have 16 truffles. Store in an airtight container in the refrigerator until ready to eat. The fat bombs will keep for 1 week in the refrigerator or 2 months in the freezer.

½ cup (68 g) whole hazelnuts (filberts) + 6 tbsp (45 g) chopped hazelnuts, divided

2 tbsp (25 g) granulated erythritol

⅓ cup (29 g) cocoa powder

½ tsp vanilla extract

⅛ tsp salt

⅓ cup (75 g) butter, cut into chunks

⅓ cup (73 g) coconut oil

Vegetarian

Prep time:
40 minutes (including setting time)

Cook time:
10 minutes

Makes 16 truffles

Weight: 0.5 oz (14 g) per truffle

Net Carbs
 1 g

Protein
1 g

Fat
13 g

123
Calories

4 g total carbs

1 g fiber

Almond Fat Bomb Fudge

2 g net carbs

These deliciously fudgy fat bomb squares are not only quick and easy to prepare but also provide a generous helping of healthy fats to keep you satiated throughout the day.

Once they have set they can be stored in the refrigerator in an airtight container, giving you instant snacks and treats throughout the week.

Line a freezer-proof 9 x 9–inch (23 x 23–cm) pan or mold with parchment paper.

Add the almond butter, coconut oil, cocoa powder, erythritol, cinnamon, ginger, vanilla and salt to a food processor. Blend well to combine, until thick and creamy. Pour the fudgy sauce into a mixing bowl.

Roughly chop the almonds into smaller chunks and add to the fudge sauce. Stir well, dispersing the almonds evenly throughout.

Pour the almond fudge mixture into the parchment-lined pan.

Transfer the pan to the freezer for a minimum of 2 hours or until set, then slice into twelve even rectangles. Store in an airtight container in the refrigerator until ready to serve. The fudge will keep for up to 1 week in the refrigerator or up to 2 months in the freezer.

¾ cup (187 g) almond butter

¾ cup (164 g) coconut oil

1 tbsp (5 g) unsweetened cocoa powder

1 tbsp (12 g) powdered erythritol

1 tsp ground cinnamon

1 tsp ground ginger

½ tsp vanilla extract

⅛ tsp salt

¼ cup (36 g) whole almonds

Vegetarian

Dairy Free

Prep time:
10 minutes +
2 hours to chill

Cook time:
None

Makes 12 rectangles

Weight: 1 oz (28 g) per rectangle

Net Carbs
 2 g

Protein
4 g

Fat
24 g

238
Calories

5 g total carbs

2 g fiber

Coconut, Lime and Raspberry Fat Bombs

1 g net carbs

These sweet and creamy fat bombs are rich with healthy fats from coconut and naturally sweet freeze-dried raspberries. These are a flavor-packed pick-me-up between meals as a sweet treat and extra fat boost.

You can use your preferred choice of low-carb sweetener in this recipe, or, as the raspberries themselves are naturally sweet, you can omit the sweetener altogether.

Add the coconut oil, coconut butter, erythritol, lime zest and 1 tablespoon (2 g) of the raspberries to a food processor. Blend until smooth and well combined.

Select a silicone mold or ice cube tray that will hold 30 fat bombs. Sprinkle a little of the remaining dried raspberries into the base of each mold.

Divide the coconut mixture evenly between the molds and transfer to the refrigerator for 30 minutes to 1 hour, until firm. The fat bombs will keep for up to 1 week in the refrigerator or up to 2 months in the freezer.

¾ cup (164 g) coconut oil

¾ cup (190 g) coconut butter

½ tbsp (6 g) powdered erythritol

1 tsp lime zest

2 tbsp (4 g) freeze-dried raspberries, divided

Keto Coach Says:

Fat bombs are a quick and easy-to-make, keto-friendly snack, and they are a handy way to increase your fat intake when you are on the go. Increasing fat intake, especially at the initial stages of your keto journey, will help stimulate your body to get in ketosis more quickly.

Vegetarian Dairy Free

 Prep time:
1 hour 15 minutes
(including setting time)

 Cook time:
None

 Makes 30 fat bombs

Weight: 0.2 oz (5.6 g)
per fat bomb

Net Carbs
 1 g

Protein
<1 g

Fat
10 g

91
Calories

 2 g total carbs

 1 g fiber

Chocolate Celebration Cake

6 g net carbs

This celebration cake is rich and moist thanks to the addition of very strongly brewed coffee. The coffee is added hot, which is the trick to getting the almond flour hydrated so the cake will be moist after baking. This is the perfect cake for a large gathering. Make sure to start baking this cake at least 4 hours before you plan to serve it, as the cake needs to cool before it is frosted.

Preheat the oven to 350°F (175°C). Lightly spray three 6-inch (15-cm) cake pans with cooking spray and line the bottoms with parchment-paper rounds. To make a parchment-paper round, cut a piece of parchment paper into a square, then fold it in quarters to make a triangle. Fold again and measure the radius of the circle by placing the folded tip in the center of the cake pan. Trim along the outside edge to match the curve of the pan, then unfold to reveal a circle that matches the size of your pan.

Combine the almond flour, erythritol, cocoa, baking powder and salt in a medium mixing bowl.

Melt the butter in a microwave-safe bowl in the microwave by heating in 30-second increments until melted. Add the vanilla to the butter. Add the butter mixture to the dry mixture and mix slightly, then add the eggs and stir again. Slowly add the hot coffee (the stronger the coffee the better!). Stir until smooth.

Divide the batter among the three cake pans.

Bake for 25 to 27 minutes, or until a toothpick inserted into the center of the cake comes out clean and the tops are puffed and slightly cracked. Allow the cake to cool completely before frosting it. The cake can be made a day ahead of time and stored in the refrigerator.

(continued)

Cake

4 cups (384 g) almond flour

1½ cups (288 g) powdered erythritol (Swerve confectioners' preferred)

1 cup (85 g) cocoa powder

2 tsp (10 g) baking powder

¼ tsp salt

1 cup (227 g) butter

2 tsp (10 ml) vanilla extract

4 large eggs

1⅓ cups (320 ml) strong, hot coffee

6+ Grams Net Carbs   Vegetarian

 Prep time:
60 minutes

 Cook time:
27 minutes + at least
2 hours cooling time

 Serves: 16

Weight: 3.5 oz (100 g) per serving

Net Carbs
 6 g

Protein
10 g

Fat
43 g

 466 Calories

 42 g total carbs

 4 g fiber

Chocolate Celebration Cake (continued)

To make the frosting, whip the cream cheese and butter in a stand mixer fitted with a paddle attachment. When fully combined, add the powdered erythritol and beat for 5 minutes, scraping down the sides as necessary, until light and fluffy. Add vanilla extract and a pinch of salt and mix again until combined, about 1 minute. Set aside at room temperature so the mixture will remain spreadable.

When ready to frost the cakes, invert the first cake onto a cake stand and remove the parchment paper. Top the cake with a generous amount of frosting and spread the frosting to the edges of the cake with an offset spatula. Invert the second cake on top of the first layer of frosting and remove the parchment. Repeat with more frosting, then invert the last layer of cake on top of the second layer.

Spread a thin layer of frosting over the whole cake. This will serve as the "crumb coat" that will hold in all the dark chocolate crumbs so the final appearance of the cake is nice and neat. Chill the cake well until the frosting is solid, about 15 minutes.

Spread the rest of the frosting evenly over the entire cake using an offset spatula. Use the spatula to create swirls of frosting on the sides of the cake.

Keep chilled. When ready to serve, allow the cake to come to room temperature for 30 minutes before serving.

Cream Cheese Frosting

16 oz (454 g) cream cheese, at room temperature

½ cup (113 g) butter, at room temperature

2 cups (384 g) powdered erythritol (Swerve confectioners' preferred)

1 tsp vanilla extract

Pinch of salt

Vanilla Cupcakes with Sour Cream Ganache

4 g net carbs

These cupcakes are moist, delicious and full of vanilla flavor. We used Lily's semi-sweet baking chips for the sugar-free chocolate chips, which makes a frosting that is not too sweet. Feel free to substitute your favorite sugar-free chocolate chips.

Preheat the oven to 350°F (175°C). Line a twelve-count cupcake pan with paper liners.

Combine the almond flour, erythritol, salt and baking powder in a medium mixing bowl.

Melt the butter in a microwave-safe bowl in the microwave in 30-second intervals until completely melted. Add the eggs and vanilla to the melted butter and stir to combine.

Heat the almond milk either in a saucepan on the stove or in a microwave-safe bowl in the microwave until very hot, 1 to 2 minutes. Add the butter and egg mixture to the dry ingredients and stir to combine, then add the hot almond milk.

Divide the batter among the twelve cupcake liners and bake for 23 to 25 minutes, until the cupcakes are lightly browned on top and cooked through. Allow the cupcakes to cool completely before frosting.

To make the frosting, set up a double boiler by placing a metal or glass bowl over a pot of simmering water. Place the chocolate chips in the bowl and slowly stir with a heat-proof spatula until the chocolate has melted. Remove the bowl from the heat and mix in the sour cream. The ganache should be thick and glossy and will start to firm as it cools.

Generously frost the cooled cupcakes and garnish each with one raspberry. Store the cupcakes in the refrigerator until ready to serve, to allow the ganache to set, about 15 minutes.

*See image on page 216.

Cupcakes

3 cups (288 g) almond flour

1 cup (240 g) powdered erythritol (Swerve confectioners' preferred)

¼ tsp salt

2 tsp (9 g) baking powder

½ cup (113 g) butter

2 large eggs

2 tsp (10 ml) vanilla extract

½ cup (120 ml) unsweetened almond milk

Frosting

8 oz (227 g) sugar-free chocolate chips

½ cup (115 g) sour cream

12 raspberries

Note:

It is easiest to frost the cupcakes within 5 minutes of making the frosting, so plan ahead and work quickly to frost the cupcakes once the ganache is ready.

Vegetarian

Prep time:
20 minutes

Cook time:
30 minutes + 30 minutes cooling time before frosting

Makes 12 cupcakes

Weight: 3.5 oz (100 g) per cupcake

Net Carbs
4 g

Protein
8 g

Fat
30 g

349
Calories

30 g total carbs

5 g fiber

Mini Chai-Spiced Cheesecakes

3 g net carbs

These kid-approved mini chai-spiced cheesecakes are perfect for a fall holiday dessert, snack or breakfast bite. Try using different spices depending on the season or your preferences. Subbing in 1 teaspoon of ground cardamom for the spice mixture and serving with fresh blueberries is great for the summer. Replace the vanilla with caramel extract and substitute 2 teaspoons (5 g) of cinnamon for the spices for a mid-winter treat. These cheesecakes store well in the refrigerator so it is worth making a batch ahead of time.

Preheat the oven to 350°F (175°C). Line a twelve-count cupcake pan with muffin liners.

To make the crust, combine the ground flax-seed, almond flour, erythritol, melted butter and salt in a mixing bowl. Spoon the mixture into the muffin liners, dividing evenly between the cups (each cup will get about 1 heaping tablespoon [15 g]) and press the mixture down firmly into each cup with the back of a spoon.

To make the cheesecakes, place the cream cheese, erythritol and salt in a medium-sized mixing bowl. Whip with a hand mixer or in a stand mixer with a paddle attachment until uniformly mixed, then add the eggs, one at a time, mixing well until combined after each addition. Add the vanilla and mix until slightly fluffy. Add the fennel, cinnamon, ginger, allspice, cardamom and cloves, and blend briefly until combined.

Divide the cream cheese among the twelve cups, using a spoon to scoop out the mixture, and a second spoon to scrape the cream cheese off of the first spoon.

Bake for 20 to 25 minutes, or until the cheesecakes are set and slightly puffed.

Allow the cheesecakes to cool slightly at room temperature, then put them in the refrigerator for at least 30 minutes to chill completely. Serve chilled.

Crust

¾ cup (78 g) ground flaxseed

¾ cup (70 g) almond flour

¼ cup (48 g) powdered erythritol (Swerve confectioners' preferred)

⅓ cup (75 g) butter, melted

⅛ tsp kosher salt

Cheesecake

16 oz (454 g) cream cheese, softened

⅔ cup (130 g) powdered erythritol (Swerve confectioners' preferred)

⅛ tsp kosher salt

3 eggs

1 tsp vanilla extract

½ tsp ground fennel

½ tsp cinnamon

1 tsp ground ginger

⅛ tsp allspice

¼ tsp ground cardamom

⅛ tsp ground cloves

Vegetarian

Prep time:
20 minutes

Cook time:
25 minutes
+ 30 minutes to chill

Makes 12 mini cheesecakes

Weight: 3.5 oz (100 g) per mini cheesecake

Net Carbs
3 g

Protein
6 g

Fat
26 g

282
Calories

17 g total carbs

3 g fiber

Pine Nut Biscotti

2 g net carbs

These cookies are made with no artificial or added sugars. They have great flavor on their own thanks to sweet and nutty pine nuts, which are toasted to perfection before being folded into the cookie dough. If you want to add a festive touch, these cookies are delicious drizzled with your choice of melted chocolate. And if a completely sweetness-free dessert is not for you, feel free to add 1 cup (192 g) of monk fruit sweetener in addition to these ingredients.

Preheat the oven to 350°F (175°C).

Place the pine nuts on an unlined baking sheet and bake for 5 minutes, until toasted. Set aside to cool.

In a medium-sized bowl, mix together the almond flour, flaxseed, coconut flour, baking powder and salt.

Add the eggs, coconut oil and vanilla and mix very well. Make sure the coconut oil is solid, but soft. There will still be visible small chunks of coconut oil, which is fine.

Fold in the toasted pine nuts.

Divide the dough in half. Place each piece on a parchment-lined baking sheet and form into a log shape, leaving a few inches between the logs.

Bake the logs for 30 minutes, or until firm. Let the logs cool completely, before using a bread knife to cut each log into ½-inch (13-mm) slices.

Place the cut cookies back on the parchment-lined baking sheet and bake for another 15 to 20 minutes, until golden brown. Store in an airtight container for up to 2 weeks.

⅓ cup (46 g) pine nuts
1⅓ cups (128 g) almond flour
2 tbsp (13 g) ground flaxseed
3 tbsp (22 g) coconut flour
1 tsp baking powder
¼ tsp kosher salt
2 large eggs
½ cup (112 g) coconut oil
1 tsp vanilla extract

Vegetarian   Dairy Free   Paleo

Prep time:
20 minutes

Cook time:
50 minutes

Makes 16 biscotti

Weight: 1 oz (28 g) per biscotti

Net Carbs
2 g

Protein
3 g

Fat
15 g

154 Calories

3 g total carbs

2 g fiber

Blackberry Crumble

6 g net carbs

These sweet blackberry and almond crumbles make the perfect quick and easy low-carb dessert, combining layers of sweet and juicy blackberries with a crisp and golden almond crumble topping.

This is a pleasing option to enjoy after Sunday lunch and can be prepared as individual portions or in one large baking dish. This crumble is perfect served with a helping of heavy cream or keto ice cream.

Preheat the oven to 325°F (165°C).

Add the blackberries to a mixing bowl with the ginger, cinnamon, erythritol and vanilla. Stir well to combine.

To prepare the topping, add the almond flour to a mixing bowl along with the erythritol and salt. Crumble in the sliced almonds, add the ground ginger and stir to combine.

Melt the coconut oil and add to the almond mixture. Stir well to form a crumble consistency.

Divide the blackberries evenly among four (3-inch [8-cm], 5-ounce [142-g]) ramekins and top each with a quarter of the crumble mixture. Alternately, place the blackberries in a 9-inch (23-cm) pie pan and top with the crumble mixture.

Transfer to the oven to bake for 18 to 20 minutes or until the fruit is bubbling and the topping is toasty and lightly golden.

Filling

2½ cups (360 g) blackberries

1 tsp ground ginger

2 tsp (5 g) ground cinnamon

2 tsp (8 g) erythritol

1 tsp vanilla extract

Crumble Topping

3 tbsp (21 g) almond flour

2 tbsp (24 g) erythritol

¼ tsp salt

2 tbsp (12 g) sliced almonds

2 tsp (5 g) ground ginger

1½ tbsp (20 g) coconut oil

6+ Grams Net Carbs

30 Minutes or Less

Vegetarian

Dairy Free

Prep time: 10 minutes

Cook time: 20 minutes

Serves: 4

Weight: 3.6 oz (102 g) per serving

Net Carbs
6 g

Protein
3 g

Fat
10 g

146 Calories

20 g total carbs

7 g fiber

Peanut Butter and Jelly Ice Cream

6 g net carbs

This deliciously creamy ice cream is quick to prep then goes straight in the freezer to set. No churning or ice cream maker required. With a classic flavor pairing of PB&J, this is a real keto crowd-pleaser! Almond butter makes a good substitute for the peanut butter.

Add the cream cheese, peanut butter, vanilla and erythritol to a food processor and blend until well combined. Alternatively, if your peanut butter is soft enough, this can be beaten together by hand.

Add the heavy cream to a mixing bowl and whisk until fluffy and soft peaks form. This can be done using a stand mixer if preferred. Add the whipped cream to the peanut butter mixture and gently fold the two together.

Add the strawberries to a food processor with 1 teaspoon of water and blend until you have a puree consistency.

Spoon half of the ice cream mixture into a freezer-proof loaf pan or dish. Drop teaspoonfuls of the strawberry puree at random over the surface of the ice cream. Gently swirl into the mixture with the spoon. Repeat this process creating a second layer with the ice cream and puree.

Cover and transfer to the freezer for 4 hours or until set. Allow the ice cream to stand and soften for a few minutes before serving.

5 oz (142 g) cream cheese, softened
⅓ cup (85 g) unsalted peanut butter
1 tsp vanilla extract
⅓ cup (65 g) powdered erythritol
1½ cups (360 ml) heavy cream
⅔ cup (95 g) strawberries

6+ Grams Net Carbs

Vegetarian

Prep time:
4 hours and 20 minutes, including freezing time

Cook time:
None

Serves: 6

Weight: 3 oz (85 g) per serving

Net Carbs
6 g

Protein
7 g

Fat
36 g

370 Calories

18 g total carbs

1 g fiber

Strawberry, Lime and Basil Granita

4 g net carbs

This light and refreshing keto dessert is packed with sweet, juicy strawberries; zesty lime and aromatic basil and is topped with a citrusy whipped cream. This is an easy-to-prepare dessert, perfect for a post-dinner treat.

Add the strawberries to a food processor along with the lime juice, basil, syrup (if using) and half of the lime zest. Blend to form a puree.

Add the water and blend again until well combined.

Pour the mixture into an approximately 9 x 13–inch (23 x 33–cm) freezer-safe tray or sheet pan and transfer to the freezer for 30 minutes to start setting.

Remove the tray from the freezer and break up the mixture with a fork, then smooth back into an even layer. Return the tray to the freezer for 30 minutes then repeat this process again. Return to the freezer for a further 30 minutes or until set and frozen solid.

Before serving, add the cream to a mixing bowl with the remaining lime zest and whisk vigorously until thick and fluffy.

Remove the granita from the freezer 5 minutes before serving to allow it to thaw a little. Break up with a fork one last time, so that you have small crystallized chunks. Divide the granita among serving bowls or glasses and top each with the lime whipped cream.

1½ cups (215 g) fresh strawberries, trimmed and sliced in half

Juice of ½ lime

2 tbsp (5 g) fresh basil

1 tbsp (15 ml) Lakanto maple-flavored syrup (or preferred low-carb sweetener; optional)

Zest of ½ lime, divided

1½ cups (360 ml) water

½ cup (120 ml) heavy cream

Vegetarian

Prep time:
15 minutes

Cook time:
2 hours (including chill time)

Serves: 4

Weight: 4.3 oz (122 g) per serving

Net Carbs
 4 g

Protein
1 g

Fat
11 g

123
Calories

 7 g total carbs

 2 g fiber

Almond Panna Cotta

3 g net carbs

This light and refreshing panna cotta has very few carbs and is delicious with no sweeteners or sugar added, although stevia is a great addition. You can make this panna cotta any flavor you would like by using different extracts. Peppermint with stevia is a favorite. To make this recipe dairy free, replace the heavy cream with a dairy-free substitute.

Sprinkle the gelatin over the cold water in a small bowl and allow the gelatin to soak for 5 minutes to soften.

Place the cream in a large saucepan and bring it to a boil over medium-high heat. Remove the pan from the heat. Pour about 1 cup (240 ml) of the cream over the gelatin and stir until fully dissolved, 2 to 3 minutes. Then, add the gelatin mixture back into the cream and stir in the almond extract and stevia drops, if using.

Place eight 4-ounce (120-ml) ramekins on a baking sheet. Divide the cream mixture evenly among the eight ramekins. Cover the ramekins with plastic wrap. Put the tray in the refrigerator to chill until firm, about 4 hours or overnight. Serve chilled.

1 (0.25-oz [7-g]) packet unflavored gelatin

¼ cup (60 ml) cold water

3 cups (710 ml) heavy cream

1 tsp almond extract

40 drops liquid stevia (optional)

Keto Coach Says:

Extracts like vanilla, banana and caramel are excellent ways to add the flavor of foods you may be craving without adding carbohydrates to a recipe. Keep a good variety of extracts in your pantry so you can enjoy the flavors that you would normally get from high-carb foods.

Prep time:
10 minutes

Cook time:
8 minutes + at least
4 hours chill time

Serves: 8

Weight: 4.5 oz (126 g) per serving

Net Carbs
3 g

Protein
3 g

Fat
32 g

308 Calories

3 g total carbs

0 g fiber

Dreamsicle Mousse

2 g net carbs

This mousse dessert tastes just like combining a dreamsicle popsicle with a slice of cheesecake! The flavors include fresh orange and vanilla. At your discretion, you can garnish with additional orange zest.

In a small bowl, whisk together the cold water and gelatin. Let it sit for 2 to 3 minutes to allow the gelatin to bloom. Then, whisk in the boiling water (you can boil more water for safety and measure out the amount you need). Set the gelatin aside for later.

In a stand mixer with a paddle attachment, whip the cream cheese until it is soft, fluffy and lump free. Mix in the vanilla and orange zest.

Transfer the cream cheese into a bowl for later and wipe your mixing bowl clean. With a whip attachment, whip the heavy cream and stevia together until you have a stiff whipped cream. Then, with the machine running, whip the gelatin mixture into the whipped cream.

Use a spatula to mix the whipped cream into the cream cheese by hand. Fold the mixture over and over gently until you have a consistent mousse (the only lumps should be the bits of orange zest).

Immediately transfer the mousse to four 5-ounce (150-ml) ramekins or small cups. You can simply spoon the mousse into the cups or use a piping bag for a more creative look. Wrap the dishes in plastic wrap and set in the refrigerator for at least 1 hour before enjoying.

1 tbsp (15 ml) cold water

1 tsp powdered gelatin

2 tbsp (30 ml) boiling water

2 oz (57 g) cream cheese, room temperature

¼ tsp vanilla extract

1 tsp orange zest

½ cup (120 ml) heavy cream

20 drops liquid stevia

Prep time:
20 minutes

Cook time:
5 minutes + 1 hour chilling time

Serves: 4

Weight: 2.2 oz (61 g) per serving

Net Carbs
2 g

Protein
3 g

Fat
16 g

156 Calories

2 g total carbs

<1 g fiber

Pantry List

If you are new to keto, this basic pantry shopping list will help you stock your pantry with 80 percent of what you need to cook the recipes in this book. Then you only need to purchase the fresh or rarely used ingredients for each recipe that you decide to cook.

Basics

Salt (kosher or sea salt)*

Black pepper

Olive oil

Avocado oil

Coconut oil

Toasted sesame oil

Apple cider vinegar

Note: I recommend choosing one type and sticking with it so that you are used to how it seasons. Table salt typically has anti-caking agents added to it and can be of a finer grain so a teaspoon ends up being "saltier." If you use it, I recommend adding less at first.

Seasonings

Chili flakes

Garlic powder

Onion powder

Cinnamon

Ground ginger

Cayenne

Cumin

Coriander

Curry powder

Paprika

Smoked paprika

Turmeric

Dried herbs (Italian seasoning, parsley, basil, thyme, rosemary)

Baking

Almond flour

Ground flaxseed

Baking soda

Baking powder

Cocoa powder

Coconut flour

Vanilla extract

Granulated Swerve (or other granulated erythritol)

Powdered Swerve (or other powdered erythritol)

Stevia (in liquid form)

Lakanto maple sweetener

Pantry

Nuts (almonds [whole, sliced and slivered], pine nuts, walnuts, hazelnuts)

Seeds (sesame, pumpkin, sunflower, chia)

Coconut (flaked and shredded)

Chicken broth

Vegetable broth

Canned coconut milk

Almond butter

Peanut butter

Tahini

Olives

Capers

Tomatoes (whole, diced, puree, sauce)**

Jarred salsa (make sure sugar is not an added ingredient)

Tuna

Anchovy fillets

**Note: I am partial to the Pomi brand of boxed tomatoes, but any tomatoes that do not contain sugar as an added ingredient are fine.*

Refrigerated

Unsweetened almond milk (or other plant-based milk— make sure there are no hidden carbohydrates)

Heavy cream

Unsalted butter

Cheeses (cream cheese, ricotta, cheddar, mozzarella, goat cheese, Parmesan)

Sour cream

Eggs

Bacon

Prosciutto

Shirataki noodles (tofu and plain)

Produce***

Avocados

Carrots

Celery

Bell peppers

Leafy greens

Lettuce

Radishes (daikon, red [salad])

Cucumbers

Green beans

Cabbage

Zucchini

Menu Ideas

Fresh herbs (parsley, cilantro, basil)

Green onions

Onion

Shallots

Ginger

Garlic

Lemons

Limes

Oranges (for zest)

Fresh berries

***Note: Some of these fresh fruits and vegetables—like carrots, celery, radishes, cabbage and citrus—will last a long time in storage, and we recommend always having them in your fridge. Others, like leafy greens and berries, are best shopped for weekly.

Condiments

Mayonnaise

Mustard

Hot sauce

Soy sauce or tamari

Fish sauce

Freezer

Chicken breasts

Shrimp

Berries

Cauliflower rice

Birthday Party Menu

Breaded Meatballs with Pesto Noodles (page 83)

Garlic-Herb Bread (page 161)

Chocolate Celebration Cake (page 225)

Thanksgiving

Orange-Glazed Cornish Hens with Broccoli Rabe (page 80)

Radish Au Gratin (page 165)

Buttermilk Biscuits (page 158)

Blackberry Crumble (page 232)

Mini Chai-Spiced Cheesecakes (page 228)

Weeknight Dinner

Citrus Salmon (page 61)

Kimchi Fried Cauli-Rice (page 166)

Seaweed Salad (page 178)

Celebration Brunch

Cucumber, Egg and Lox Bites (page 211)

Bacon, Cheese and Watercress Omelettes (page 36)

Cinnamon-Flax Almond Muffins (page 28)

Very Berry Tea (page 51)

References

[1] N. B. Bueno, I. S. de Melo, S. L. de Oliveira, and T. da Rocha Ataide. "Very-low-carbohydrate ketogenic diet v. low-fat diet for long-term weight loss: a meta-analysis of randomised controlled trials." *British Journal of Nutrition* 110, no. 7 (2013): 1178–87. doi:10.1017/S0007114513000548.

[2] S. J. Athinarayanan et al. "Long-Term Effects of a Novel Continuous Remote Care Intervention Including Nutritional Ketosis for the Management of Type 2 Diabetes: A 2-Year Non-randomized Clinical Trial." *Frontiers in Endocrinology (Lausanne)* 10 (2019): 348. doi:10.3389/fendo.2019.00348.

[3] A. F. Cicero, M. Benelli, M. Brancaleoni, G. Dainelli, D. Merlini, and R. Negri. "Middle and Long-Term Impact of a Very Low-Carbohydrate Ketogenic Diet on Cardiometabolic Factors: A Multi-Center, Cross-Sectional, Clinical Study." *High Blood Pressure & Cardiovascular Prevention* 22, no. 4 (2015): 389–94. doi:10.1007/s40292-015-0096-1.

[4] P. Puchalska and P. A. Crawford. "Multi-dimensional Roles of Ketone Bodies in Fuel Metabolism, Signaling, and Therapeutics." *Cell Metabolism* 25, no. 2 (2017): 262–84. doi:10.1016/j.cmet.2016.12.022.

[5] Y. H. Youm et al. "The ketone metabolite beta-hydroxybutyrate blocks NLRP3 inflammasome-mediated inflammatory disease." *Nature Medicine* 21, no. 3 (2015): 263–69. doi:10.1038/nm.3804.

[6] A. Gyorkos, M. H. Baker, L. N. Miutz, D. A. Lown, M. A. Jones, and L. D. Houghton-Rahrig. "Carbohydrate-restricted Diet and Exercise Increase Brain-derived Neurotrophic Factor and Cognitive Function: A Randomized Crossover Trial." *Cureus* 11, no. 9 (2019): e5604. doi:10.7759/cureus.5604.

[7] M. Ota et al. "Effect of a ketogenic meal on cognitive function in elderly adults: potential for cognitive enhancement." *Psychopharmacology* 233, no. 21–22 (2016): 3797–802. doi:10.1007/s00213-016-4414-7.

[8] A. I. Castro et al. "Effect of A Very Low-Calorie Ketogenic Diet on Food and Alcohol Cravings, Physical and Sexual Activity, Sleep Disturbances, and Quality of Life in Obese Patients." *Nutrients* 10, no. 10 (2018). doi:10.3390/nu10101348.

[9] J. Volek et al. "Comparison of energy-restricted very low-carbohydrate and low-fat diets on weight loss and body composition in overweight men and women." *Nutrition & Metabolism (Lond)* 1, no. 1 (2004): 13. doi:10.1186/1743-7075-1-13.

[10] J. S. Volek, T. Noakes, and S. D. Phinney. "Rethinking fat as a fuel for endurance exercise." *European Journal of Sport Science* 15, no. 1 (2015): 13–20. doi:10.1080/17461391.2014.959564.

[11] R. M. Krauss, P. J. Blanche, R. S. Rawlings, H. S. Fernstrom, and P. T. Williams. "Separate effects of reduced carbohydrate intake and weight loss on atherogenic dyslipidemia." *The American Journal of Clinical Nutrition* 83, no. 5 (2006): 1025–31. doi:10.1093/ajcn/83.5.1025.

[12] J. S. Volek et al. "Metabolic characteristics of keto-adapted ultra-endurance runners." *Metabolism* 65, no. 3 (2016): 100–10. doi:10.1016/j.metabol.2015.10.028.

[13] W. C. Kephart et al. "The Three-Month Effects of a Ketogenic Diet on Body Composition, Blood Parameters, and Performance Metrics in CrossFit Trainees: A Pilot Study." *Sports (Basel)* 6, no. 1 (2018). doi:10.3390/sports6010001.

[14] T. Dostal, D. J. Plews, P. Hofmann, P. B. Laursen, and L. Cipryan. "Effects of a 12-Week Very-Low Carbohydrate High-Fat Diet on Maximal Aerobic Capacity, High-Intensity Intermittent Exercise, and Cardiac Autonomic Regulation: Non-randomized Parallel-Group Study." *Frontiers in Physiology* 10 (2019): 912. doi:10.3389/fphys.2019.00912.

Acknowledgments

I want to say a giant thank you to our amazing community of Carb Manager users—it is only with your support and feedback that Carb Manager has been able to become the #1 keto diet app.

Thanks to the entire Carb Manager team—especially Melisa Navarro, Trever Clark and Gabriela Preiss who had a hand in making this cookbook come to life—for all your hard work shipping code, rewriting SOPs and keeping spirits up by posting cute pet pics. Thanks to Anthony O'Neill and Anna Rose Dornier for your contributions and quick replies to my numerous questions. A special thank you to Emma Carter, Jessica Lewandowski and Amanda Vuu, our talented recipe writers who I worked with on this cookbook and who are responsible for building our library of delicious keto recipes.

Thank you to everyone at Page Street Publishing for working with us to create this cookbook, especially our editor, Sarah Monroe. To everyone in my writing group and cookbook club: Your support and friendship has meant so much to me. Elicia Johnson and Stephanie Sandleben, thank you for your careful reading and helpful suggestions.

Thank you to my children and my parents, Marvin and Lani Davis. I appreciate your help testing recipes and giving unvarnished feedback. Finally, a huge thank you to my husband, Kevin Yip, the founder of Carb Manager. You are an inspiration to all of us.

About the Author

Since 2010, Carb Manager has been the #1 low-carb and keto diet tracker for iOS, Android and the web. Carb Manager's mission is to make the low-carb lifestyle easy, fun and delicious and empower our millions of members to achieve their wellness goals.

Mandy Davis is the co-founder of Carb Manager. After receiving her undergraduate degree in English Literature at Harvard University, she attended the Seattle Culinary Academy, and has worked as a restaurant critic, cookbook reviewer, cook on a boat in Alaska, baker, line cook and high school English teacher. She lives with her family on an island in the Puget Sound.

Index